Real Life Financial Planning for the New Physician

A Resident, Fellow, and Young Physician's Guide to Financial Security

Todd D. Bramson & Marshall W. Gifford

BOOK IDEA SUBMISSIONS

If you are a C-level executive or senior lawyer interested in submitting a book idea or manuscript to the Aspatore editorial board, please e-mail authors@aspatore.com. Aspatore is especially looking for highly specific book ideas that would have a direct financial impact on behalf of a reader. Completed books can range from 20 to 2,000 pages—the topic and "need to read" aspect of the material are most important, not the length. Include your book idea, biography, and any additional pertinent information.

SPEAKER SUBMISSIONS FOR CONFERENCES

If you are interested at giving a speech for an upcoming ReedLogic conference (a partner of Aspatore Books), please e-mail the ReedLogic Speaker Board at speakers@reedlogic.com. If selected, speeches are given over the phone and recorded (no travel necessary). Due to the busy schedules and travel implications for executives, ReedLogic produces each conference on CD-ROM, then distributes the conference to bookstores and executives who register for the conference. The finished CD-ROM includes the speaker picture with the audio of the speech playing in the background, similar to a radio address played on television.

INTERACTIVE SOFTWARE SUBMISSIONS

If you have an idea for an interactive business or software legal program, please e-mail software@reedlogic.com. ReedLogic is especially looking for Excel spreadsheet models and PowerPoint presentations that help business professionals and lawyers achieve specific tasks. If idea or program is accepted, product is distributed to bookstores nationwide.

ISBN 1-59622-292-1

Library of Congress Control Number: 2001012345

Managing Editor, Leah M. Jones, Edited by Eddie Fournier, Cover design by Tasha Kelter

About Aspatore Books –
Publishers of C-Level Business Intelligence

www.Aspatore.com
Aspatore Books is the largest and most exclusive publisher of C-level executives (CEO, CFO, CTO, CMO, partner) from the world's most respected companies and law firms. Aspatore annually publishes a select group of C-level executives from the Global 1,000, top 250 law firms (partners and chairs), and other leading companies of all sizes. C-Level Business Intelligence™, as conceptualized and developed by Aspatore Books, provides professionals of all levels with proven business intelligence from industry insiders—direct and unfiltered insight from those who know it best—as opposed to third-party accounts offered by unknown authors and analysts. Aspatore Books is committed to publishing an innovative line of business and legal books, those which lay forth principles and offer insights that when employed, can have a direct financial impact on the reader's business objectives, whatever they may be. In essence, Aspatore publishes critical tools—need-to-read as opposed to nice-to-read books—for all business professionals.

Dedications

This book is dedicated to my immediate family. Without the love, support, and guidance of all of them, I wouldn't have learned the most important lesson of life. That is..."When all is said and done, it is the quality and depth of relationships and experiences that are the essence of life...not the accumulation of material possessions."

— Todd D. Bramson

This book is dedicated to my entire family, especially my wife Tari, who has supported me while I built my practice and provides support on a daily basis. Also, I thank my parents, who taught me that "anything is possible if you have confidence in yourself." I would also like to dedicate this to my clients, who have trusted me and helped me gain the knowledge included in this book.

— Marshall W. Gifford

Thank You

We extend a special thank you to …

… our clients, who have trusted us with their financial decisions

… our staff, specifically Jennifer Lange, Greg Halat, and Kelly Cherwien

… our partners Eric Seybert, Brett VanderBloemen, Greg Wikelius, Brian Hensen, and Josh Evenson

… our business associates, who make work a pleasure

Background and Motivation

I have gained wisdom, strength of character, integrity, empathy, and the value of giving by my parents' example. Unfortunately, my father passed away very suddenly at the age of forty-five, when I was just sixteen. It was only three weeks from the day he discovered a few black and blue marks on his arms to the day he died of acute leukemia. In this short time, we never had a chance to talk about the future, although I feel his guidance through my conscience and in the wisdom of others, including my mother.

It is interesting how the experiences of childhood, both good and bad, mold the path we follow as adults. My dad did not have much life insurance, or any established relationships with trusted advisors. When he died, my mother was lost financially. She was given very poor financial advice, and the small amount of life insurance she had was lost in an unsuitable and inappropriate investment. My family's misfortune defined my passion. It was through this unfortunate situation that I became empowered. My mission has remained intact for more than twenty-five years, as I decided this would never happen to my family or anyone who entrusted me with their important financial decisions.

Todd D. Bramson

I grew up in a small town in Northeast Iowa. My parents were both successful business owners. My father ran an insurance agency, and my mother ran an antique and gift shop. It wasn't until 1989, during my senior year of high school, that I learned how quickly life can change. In February of 1989, I was diagnosed with Lupus Nephritis, a disease of the autoimmune system. In the middle of basketball season and recruiting trips, my season ended. At 6' 4", my weight dropped to 126 pounds. The next seven months I spent in and out of hospitals. I was very fortunate to fully recover physically in late 1989, and have been healthy for the past fifteen years. The experience, however, will never be forgotten. It serves as a reminder to make sure I take care of those closest to me and live every day, because you never know when life will deviate from your plan.

Marshall W. Gifford

The title of this book is *Real Life Financial Planning for the New Physician*. We do not live life in a controlled environment. The best you can do is plan thoughtfully and thoroughly, factoring in all the potential outcomes.

We would like to share a proverb containing some valuable wisdom and insight:

He (or she) who knows, and knows he knows, is wise;
Follow him.
He who knows, but knows not that he knows, is asleep;
Awaken him.
He who knows not, and knows he does not know, is simple;
Teach him.
He who knows not, but does not know that he knows not, is dangerous;
Avoid him.

We believe it's our mission in life to listen to and learn from, or **follow**, those who fall into the first category. But it is also our mission to take our unique gifts and make them available to those who are asleep or simple by **awakening** and **teaching** them. Also, time is too precious to spend with those who are dangerous. **Avoid** and minimize the amount of time you spend with people who fall into this category, and your enjoyment of life will multiply. We all have unique gifts and abilities, and to the extent that our lives overlap and intertwine, we can all grow together carrying out our unique visions.

It is our hope that this book will educate and motivate you to achieve all of your personal and financial goals.

Todd D. Bramson and Marshall W. Gifford

Real Life Financial Planning for the New Physician

CONTENTS

1	INTRODUCTION	13
2	WHERE DO I START?	21
3	THE PYRAMID	29
4	THE SECURITY AND CONFIDENCE STAGE: EMERGENCY FUNDS	35
5	DEBT MANAGEMENT	39
6	RISK MANAGEMENT, INSURANCE, AND ASSET PROTECTION	45
7	THE CAPITAL ACCUMULATION STAGE	61
8	THE TAX- ADVANTAGED STAGE	67
9	THE SPECULATION STAGE	81
10	CONTRACTS, AGREEMENTS, AND OTHER CONSIDERATIONS	83
11	CONCLUSION	89

12 **ADDITIONAL RESOURCES** **91**

ABOUT THE AUTHORS **99**

1

Introduction

Why the title, *Real Life Financial Planning for the New Physician?*

Quite simply, residents, fellows, and young physicians have unique financial needs. You have so many financial issues and options on a personal and business level. This complexity can make decision making very difficult. With our thirty years of combined experience catering to the medical profession, we have not seen a resource like this book.

Our experience reveals that most physicians have a significant interest in financial issues, but many are simply too busy to take the time to learn what they need to know. During school, residency, and/or fellowship, the focus is on your training, and few curriculums teach financial planning. There may be a class on practice management or contracts, but none that really address the actual details of a financial plan for you or your practice.

Upon completion of training, your time is now spent getting established in a practice. In addition, many of you will get married and start a family, which can delay financial planning even longer. Before you know it, years have gone by and still...no financial plan.

If you have a comprehensive plan—congratulations. This book can serve as a reference to reinforce what you are doing. But like high cholesterol that can't be ignored, you must begin immediately to initiate your financial plan. This book will give you the start you need.

There is so much information "out there," but sometimes not much wisdom. This book summarizes the wisdom we have gained and shared with our clients in individual meetings throughout the years. *Real Life Financial Planning for the New Physician* is simply a practical method of understanding, organizing, and prioritizing financial decisions.

Most financial planning publications, and financial plans themselves, assume everyone lives a long, healthy life and saves a good portion of their income in quality investments that always do well. This book addresses the issues that happen in **real life**, good and bad.

A solid financial plan should make your life simpler by letting you focus on the issues you excel at and enjoy. This may include practicing medicine, spending time with your family, or pursuing hobbies. These activities are more enjoyable knowing that your finances are in order. We hope you take the time to read this book and work with a trained professional to develop and implement a financial plan that meets *your* goals and objectives.

As a young physician, you wear many hats, especially if you are self-employed or a partner in a practice. With that in mind, surrounding yourself with advisors that can help you is crucial to your success. We recommend you have the following specialists on your team:

Your Advisory Team

Financial Advisor – Your financial advisor is often the quarterback of the entire team. They can help organize and prioritize all of your goals and objectives, both business and personal. A comprehensive plan is developed, which coordinates your risk management, savings, retirement, debt management, and tax reduction needs.

Banker – The banker's role will be to arrange financing for buying a private practice. A banker can also help you finance a new building or surgical center, and the necessary equipment. The banker will also help determine the most favorable loan terms. On a personal level, the banker can help with loan consolidations and mortgage financing, as well as cash management accounts.

Attorney – Initially, an attorney may help you review your contract. Then when you buy a house, an attorney should review those documents. Along the way, an attorney will help you draft legal documents such as wills and trusts. As your net worth grows, select an attorney who is an expert in asset protection strategies specific to the state you live in.

Accountant – An accountant will not only make sure you are properly filing your tax returns, but he or she may also assist you in setting up bookkeeping systems, practice valuation, compensation formulas, and payroll services, as well as depreciating and expensing equipment if you have your own practice.

Financial success isn't, as most people might suspect, the ability to make one or two decisions that turn a buck into a million. Rather, financial success is the result of many small but sound decisions that, when compounded, add up to substantial financial security.

You are in complete control…or at least you should be. When it comes to spending and saving, investing and paying taxes, many may offer good advice, but you're the only one who can do anything about it. Maybe you're unsure of your investment options and how to prioritize them. Maybe you don't have a clue where your paycheck goes each month. In any case, if you're reading this book, you already understand the importance of getting your future under control, and that's the crucial first step to financial freedom.

Financial independence and the accumulation of wealth are no accident. Granted, it's not possible to plan for every single event in life, but even tragedy can feel more manageable when you are financially prepared for it. *Many people spend more time planning for a family vacation than for their financial future!* Whether it's preparing for the future, planning for the transition of your business, insuring your family against tragedy, or planning for the good times, your money deserves your undivided attention.

Car accidents, marriage, divorce, children, changing practices, death, retirement, taxes, for better or worse, are the realities of life. Planning for any circumstance, both happy and sad, may seem like a burden right now, but the proper planning will rescue you when (not if) unforeseen circumstances arise.

The truth is we all need to plan for our financial futures. The question is not whether to plan, but how to go about making a plan, and whether you need a professional to help.

Also, the information age has intensified the field of financial planning. It is interesting to consider that twenty years ago, financial news may have made top headlines two or three times throughout the year when the stock market would do particularly poorly or well, or if there was some other major economic news. Today, however, we have news programs dedicated to nothing else twenty-four hours a day, seven days week, and the number of financial headlines in the daily papers can be overwhelming. Still, there is a big difference between information and wisdom, and that's where the insight of a trusted professional can help.

Should You Hire a Financial Planner?

Several situations that may call for a financial planner's expertise are:

- *You are very busy without much spare time.* In this case, a financial planner can save you a bit of your most precious commodity—time.
- *You are easily bored or overwhelmed by financial questions.* If, for example, preparing a budget is such a nuisance that you can't even imagine having to sort through anything more complex, then hiring a financial planner may be money well spent for greater peace of mind.
- *You are considering a complicated set of employee benefits in combination with personally owned insurance and investments.* You don't want your new benefits to conflict or overlap with your current

investments and insurance. A careful review will avoid gaps and/or duplication.

- *You have recently graduated from school and started your residency, or just finished a residency and are suddenly expected to manage a much higher income.* The saying "an ounce of prevention is worth a pound of cure" is an important one in the world of financial planning. Seemingly insurmountable debt plagues the future of many young physicians. Learning whether you should consolidate your student loans, budgeting properly, choosing insurance options, and making wise investments are necessary life skills. Getting professional advice **now** beats paying for costly mistakes later.

- *You are self employed.* In this case, you most likely have to "wear many hats" as an entrepreneur. You are the physician, the marketer, the practice manager, and probably don't have time to investigate or be aware of the many planning options available to you and your employees. A financial planner can help you sort through the many issues facing you.

The topic doesn't matter, whether it's religion, politics, stocks, insurance, sales loads, or how to finance your house, just to name a few. There are always many individual considerations, and the correct solution depends on a variety of factors. We get leery of advice that suggests you should "always" do this or "never" do that. We believe life, as well as most financial decisions is more gray, than black or white.

We are not the first to say this, and we certainly won't be the last: *"It is crucial to trust your own judgment and instinct before taking action, no matter how good someone makes their argument."* The best way to gain confidence in your own judgment is to educate yourself on the topic at hand.

Have you thought about any of the following questions?

- How much money should I have in emergency reserves?
- Should I consolidate my student loans?
- In which order should I go about paying off my debt?

- What is the right kind of insurance for me, and how much do I need?
- What insurance should I have for my practice?
- How should I go about setting up a savings plan?
- What are my investment options?
- What is the best type of retirement plan for me and my employees?
- How should I plan for college education for my children?
- How much do I need to save to retire?
- How do I protect my assets in the event of a lawsuit?
- What tax-sheltered options are available to me?
- How do I establish a budget?
- What are the most common financial mistakes people make?

If you don't know the answers, just keep reading, because you're about to find out.

As a medical professional, you face significant transitions. At each one, it is critical that you take the appropriate steps. The major transitions for all physicians are from medical school to residency, and from residency to practice. The third key transition facing some is becoming a partner in a practice. Each of these transitions poses its own unique challenges, and planning opportunities.

We will discuss all these issues in more detail throughout the book, but to summarize, as you transition from medical school to residency, the key issues to address are:

- Consolidate your student loans to lock in your interest rate.
- Fund a Roth IRA if cash flow allows. You will be unable to fund it once you enter practice due to the income restrictions on the Roth IRA.
- Purchase an individual occupation-specific disability policy to protect yourself and your family in the event of a disability. Most training programs offer group disability of 60 to 80 percent of your

salary, which is not enough to cover your loan payments and house or rent payments. It is imperative that if you are unable to work that you are still able to make your payments and still have money left to live.

- Obtain an inexpensive convertible term life policy to protect your family and your insurability. The cost is normally around $30 to $50 per month per million of coverage.
- Consider purchasing a home if your program is longer than three years.
- Purchase an umbrella liability policy of at least $1 million to protect your assets against lawsuits arising from personal negligence or the acts of others. The cost of this is normally $100 to $150 **per year**. As your net worth increases, raise your umbrella liability coverage to the maximum you can get.
- Draft a will and appoint guardians and trustees if you have minor children.

The goal in residency or fellowship is to guard against catastrophic financial problems, protect your insurability, initiate a basic savings program and educate yourself so that you can become financially independent as efficiently as possible once you enter practice.

At the conclusion of residency or fellowship, you should:

- Set your financial parameters and determine your key financial goals.
- Implement a plan with your increased income to accomplish your financial goals.
- Allocate at least 20 percent of your income to debt reduction or asset accumulation.
- Begin contributions to pretax retirement plan such as 401(k)'s, 403(b)'s, 457 plans or other qualified plans through your practice.
- Increase your disability insurance.
- Review your life insurance to make sure it is maximized.
- Establish an asset protection plan.

- Establish a debt reduction strategy.

Each time you receive a significant raise, make sure you set a portion aside for your financial priorities. If you save 20 percent or more of your income, you should be financially independent within twenty-five years. Getting in the habit of saving early is much easier than adjusting to your new income and then trying to cut expenses in the future. At your age, it is important to periodically review your goals to make sure you are still on track. We suggest that once or twice a year is normally sufficient.

2

Where Do I Start?

Your Net Worth Statement

The starting point of any financial plan is to calculate your current net worth. This is a snapshot of what you are worth at an exact point in time. In order to determine your net worth, you simply add up all of your assets and subtract all of your liabilities (debts). Often, when you are just starting out, the net worth is actually a negative number, because the liabilities exceed the assets.

In order to measure your financial progress, it is important to know your net worth. Many people measure their financial progress by how much money they have in the bank. In reality, as the value of your assets go up, such as a house, business, or investments, and as you pay debts down, your net worth may be increasing more dramatically than you think. The most important way to measure financial progress is to calculate your net worth regularly. After you learn how to do it once, it will be easy.

In simple terms, what would you be worth if you sold everything you owned and turned it into cash, then paid off all your debts? If this is the first time you're preparing a net worth statement, it's also a good idea to try and estimate what you think your net worth has been over the last few years. Hopefully, you will be pleasantly surprised at the progress you've made.

There are several categories within the net worth statement.

Fixed assets is the first category, and includes those assets that do not have a risk of a loss of principal. These include very conservative assets. A few examples would be checking and savings accounts, money market funds, certificates of deposit, T-bills, EE savings bonds, and whole life insurance cash values. These would be assets you have access to in an emergency, and they are available now, so they are considered liquid.

Variable assets include most other financial assets. Examples include stocks, bonds, mutual funds, retirement plans, or any investment where the principal can fluctuate.

Your personal and/or other assets would include tangible assets such as your house, personal or business property, and vehicles. Other tangible assets, such as a boat, computer, and camera, would also be included here.

Don't get too bogged down trying to establish a value for every piece of personal property. You may already have that information available from your homeowner's or renter's insurance policies, but if not, a rough estimate will work just fine. The main reason for gathering this information is to have an estimate so you can monitor trends. This way, when you are reviewing your net worth after some time, you will be able to track how this category has changed or account for some of the money you spent.

*Tip: Use a video camera to film each room in your house, including closets and the garage. In the event of a loss, it will be much easier to remember for the insurance company's reporting purposes.

Fixed Assets:

Savings Account:	$15,000
Checking Account:	$3,000
Certificate of Deposit:	$2,000
Total:	**$20,000**

Variable Assets:

IRA:	$13,000
Roth IRA:	$9,000
Mutual Funds:	$10,000
Individual Stocks:	$2,000
Variable Life Cash Value:	$4,000
401(k) Balance:	$40,000
Total:	**$78,000**

Personal and Other Assets:

Home:	$375,000
Vehicle:	$20,000
Personal Property:	$30,000
Total:	**$425,000**

Total Assets: **$523,000**

Liabilities:

Mortgage:	$290,000
Home Equity Line:	$35,000
Vehicle Loan:	$10,000
Credit Cards:	$2,000
Student Loans:	$110,000
Total:	**$447,000**

Net Worth

(Assets Minus Liabilities):   **$76,000**

For your *liabilities*, list the amount you would owe if you could pay off the amount today, not the total of the payments over time, which include interest. Don't forget to include all loans like mortgages, auto loans, credit cards, student loans, personal debts, and consumer loans.

Subtract your total liabilities from your assets to arrive at your net worth. For many people, this can be a sobering experience. Keep in mind that it is typical for new physicians to have a negative net worth due to substantial student loans. However, your education is an investment in your financial future. Where else could you have invested $150,000 and expect a return of $100,000+ each year for the next thirty years?

If your net worth is negative, your first financial goal is to get your net worth back to zero. This can be done by reducing debt or accumulating assets. For you, it is especially important to establish a financial plan and get control of your financial life as soon as possible.

The Millionaire Next Door, by Thomas Stanley, outlines some benchmark figures for what your net worth should be at any given time, age, or stage in life. Your net worth represents your financial security and, ultimately, financial independence. So, of course, the closer you are to retirement, the higher your net worth should be. A successful financial plan achieves one's maximum net worth, works under all circumstances, and optimizes the enjoyment of your wealth. It will also be important to insure yourself against unforeseen tragedies and to consider whether you want to leave an inheritance to your family or your favorite charity, establishing a legacy that lives on after you.

In summary, the most critical starting point to a financial plan is evaluating your net worth. Then, on a periodic basis, you can compare the results in order to establish trends and measure improvement. A convenient time to do this is once a year when you're doing your taxes. This way, all the paperwork is readily available and you're focused on your annual earnings and expenditures. Keep all the financial records together from each year's tax forms and net worth calculations for easy reference.

Your Budget

After calculating your net worth, look at your monthly expenses and determine where your money is being spent.

For most people, the thought of budgeting is painful. In our opinion, the benefits of having a successful financial future outweigh the frustrating budgeting process. It is very important to know, generally, where your money goes. It is helpful to track expenses to see if there are inefficiencies in your business or personal habits or hobbies that cost more than you think.

Any successful financial plan requires an understanding of your cash flow so you can establish systematic savings to retirement funds, college funds, debt payoffs, or emergency funds. We have found that if you set up an automated savings of 70 to 80 percent of your surplus cash flow, your household finances should function smoothly. The example below assumes an income of around $210,000. Obviously, during your training, your income will not be as high. Most residents and fellows take home between $2,000 and $2,800 per month, depending on your year in the program.

Example:

Monthly after-tax income:	$12,000
Monthly expenses:	$8,000
Surplus:	$4,000

It should be easy to save $2,800 per month automatically (70 percent of $4,000 = $2,800).

To determine your surplus, it is helpful to track your income and expenses for a couple of months.

Sample Budget

Net Income After Taxes:	$_____

subtract

Mortgage or Rent:	$_____
Car Payment:	$_____
Student Loans:	$_____
Groceries:	$_____
Travel:	$_____
Entertainment/Meals Out:	$_____
Insurances:	$_____
Utilities:	$_____
Phones:	$_____
Clothing:	$_____
Child Care:	$_____
Health Care:	$_____
Internet:	$_____
Gifts:	$_____
Dues:	$_____
Charitable Contributions:	$_____
Miscellaneous:	$_____

This remainder equals your surplus:	$_____

Many people overlook the miscellaneous expenses. These expenses individually are not significant, but added together can be quite large. Examples of these are home repairs, veterinary bills, haircuts, clothing, oil changes, car repairs, household items, lunches out, coffee, diapers, etc. To get a good idea of your miscellaneous expenses, you may want to carry around a pocket calendar for a month or two and write down the money you spend.

Once you have a good idea what your monthly inflows and outflows are, automate your savings. Treat your investment amount as a bill you pay every month. Our experience shows that if you don't get in the habit of saving money on a regular basis, either through a payroll deduction or an automatic withdrawal from you checking account, the money you intended to go toward savings or investments is simply spent elsewhere. Initially, it is not the amount being saved that is important, but the habit being formed!

The following chart illustrates the importance of developing the habit of saving as soon as you can. The monthly savings amount is what would be needed to be saved starting at that age to accumulate $1,000,000 by age sixty-five at 8 and 10 percent net rates of return.

Age	Monthly Savings Amount	
	10%	8%
25	$158	$287
35	$492	$671
45	$1,316	$1,698
55	$4,882	$5,467

To further demonstrate the importance of the compounding of capital over time, here is the result of saving $10,000 per year at 9 percent into a tax-deferred account:

Age to Start	Account Balance at Age 65
25	$3,682,918
35	$1,485,752
45	$557,645
55	$165,602

Both tables illustrate the power of compound interest. Even small amounts early in life can have a huge impact on your retirement account balances. We strongly recommend that as you transition from school to your practice, you immediately set some important financial goals. Write down what is important to you. This could be retiring at age fifty-five, paying off school loans by age thirty-five, funding college for two children, owning a practice in three years, or having a second home in ten years. Determine what type of financial commitment those goals require, and establish the appropriate investment accounts for your goals.

Generally speaking, if you start saving in your late twenties, a savings rate of 15 percent of your gross income should be enough to keep you safe from financial worries at retirement. If you are getting a later start in your mid-thirties, then you may need to be saving 20 to 25 percent. If you have accounted for your long-term financial security, it makes spending the remainder more rewarding by eliminating the guilt or fear many people feel in their day–to-day finances, or when making large purchases.

3

The Pyramid

If you took a jigsaw puzzle and dumped all the pieces on the table, it is initially a daunting task to begin to put the puzzle together. Grab a puzzle piece out of the pile at random, and it's hard to know where that piece fits into the big picture. It is much easier to put the puzzle together if you have a picture of what the scene will look like once completed. So, you look at the picture on the box to give you a guide to what the puzzle looks like when completed. We designed the pyramid as a method of seeing how a properly designed financial plan looks when it is put together correctly.

The pyramid is a method of explaining the financial planning concept by categorizing your financial plan into stages. Of course, individual goals, habits, accomplishments, etc. are all unique, but most people share the same fundamental life stages. As a method of efficiently organizing your financial life, the pyramid represents the key to financial independence, and demonstrates the basic goal of increasing your assets and reducing your debt in order to have enough money invested to retire comfortably. Individuals may place more or less importance on one section of the pyramid than another, which is perfectly acceptable.

Without a doubt, organizing your finances in order to build a solid base is the first step. If you do not do this, you may be subjecting your financial situation to undue risk, which will cause problems later on. On the other hand, it's also important not to place too much emphasis on only one stage, neglecting the overall balance. This could be a sign of being overly conservative. As an example, not taking advantage of higher potential returns in equity (stock) or real estate investments may mean losing your purchasing power in the long run, because the dollars may be worth less, due to the effects of taxes and inflation.

It is very important to try and accomplish a lifelong financial balance. You certainly don't want to scrimp all your life and get to the age of sixty-five with a large amount of money saved, only to be in poor health and not be able to enjoy it. By the same token, you don't want to be nearing retirement and realize you haven't saved enough and now must take a substantial drop in your standard of living or continue to practice longer than you wanted to. The ideal situation would be to retire at the same or a greater standard of living than you were accustomed to while practicing, but not feel at any time that you have greatly sacrificed.

A fundamental of short-term and long-term financial success is living on less than your income. If you can get used to living on 80 percent of your income, this allows you to commit 20 percent of your income to your net worth. Initially, this may mean aggressively paying off loans, but over time, the majority of this extra income should be saved.

As you can see by the diagram, there are four main stages to the financial planning pyramid: the *Security and Confidence Stage*, the *Capital Accumulation Stage*, the *Tax-Advantaged Stage*, and the *Speculation Stage*.

The ideal investment is completely liquid and has lots of tax advantages, a high rate of return, and low risk. If you find an advisor or salesman claiming to have such an investment, you would be wise to avoid them, as they are dangerous. This ideal investment does not exist. Let's use an analogy of spinning plates. If you have ever been to a circus or seen a juggler, you may have seen a performer attempt to spin a lot of plates on long sticks—all at the same time. The objective is to take limited energy, and allocate it in such a manner as to keep all the plates spinning. It doesn't do any good to devote a lot of time to one spinning plate while the others are slowing down, wobbling, and falling down. The goal is to keep all the plates spinning!

PYRAMID OF FINANCIAL NEEDS

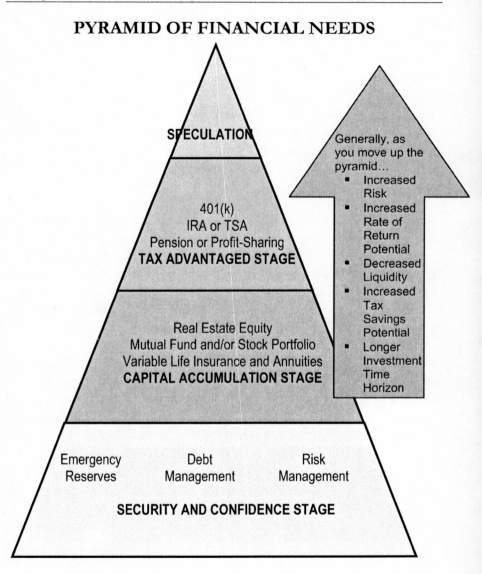

Your financial plan is on somewhat the same level, with each financial decision representing a different plate. First of all, you need to find out which plates you want to start spinning, and then direct your dollars to keep them going. You could have several debt reduction plates, some risk management (insurance) plates, retirement and/or college education plates, and so on. Each individual situation is going to be different. Again, there are limited resources that need to be allocated in such a way as to accomplish all of your goals. This is where the advice of a professional and experienced financial advisor can be very valuable.

The key financial variables in the pyramid are risk, liquidity, rate of return, and tax advantages. The money in your emergency reserves and at the *Security and Confidence Stage* should be very liquid or accessible. Generally, as you move to higher stages in the pyramid, the less liquid your funds become.

Risk and rate of return tend to go hand in hand. The higher the amount of risk you take, the higher the rate of return should be, **given time**. In the pyramid, lower risk with lower rates of return should be at the base of your planning. The risk and rate of return increase as you move up the pyramid. Historically, stock market and investing returns become more predictable the longer the timeframe that is considered. Keep in mind, however, that past performance is not indicative of future results.

At the lower level of the financial pyramid, there are typically not many tax advantages. If you have money in a savings account, that money is generating ordinary income on which you are paying taxes each year. On the other hand, when you put money into a qualified retirement plan, the contribution is on a before tax basis, delaying and deferring the tax to a later date. Under most circumstances, however, you cannot touch the money in your qualified plan until age fifty-nine-and-a-half without paying a 10 percent early withdrawal penalty, plus the income taxes due on that amount. The rule of thumb on tax savings is similar to risk and rate of return. As you move up the pyramid, you'll have greater tax advantages on your investments.

A Discussion of Risk

There is no such thing as a risk-free investment; even a savings account is not risk-free. Let us explain. Risk is commonly discussed in terms of loss of principal. During the recent bear market (a period of downturn in the stock market), many investors lost some of the value of their investment if they owned stocks and/or stock mutual funds. There are other forms of risk besides market risk.

Purchasing Power Risk: Another term for this is inflation. If the cost for products and services rises faster than the interest rate being credited on your savings and checking accounts, then you are exposed to purchasing power risk. While you don't lose any principal, you are still losing ground relative to inflation. This is a particular problem currently for retirees who have traditionally held CDs and lived off the interest each year.

Interest Rate Risk: Bonds and fixed income securities are subject to this risk. Your principal value can decline if interest rates climb quickly. The severity of the loss is often magnified by the duration and/or maturity of the bonds and the credit quality. At this time, when interest rates are near forty-year lows, many people who own fixed income securities are unknowingly subjecting their investments to interest rate risk.

Business Risk: This is the risk of losing money due to circumstances out of your control. A business could go bankrupt, and your investment becomes worthless.

Liquidity Risk: This is the risk associated with being invested in real estate, limited partnerships, businesses, and other investments where there is sometimes no immediate market for your value. This is problematic if you have a need for cash and you cannot sell or liquidate your shares. You would invest in something like this only if you had sufficient assets available besides this investment.

Regulatory Risk: Investors run the risk that government policy decisions or influences of society as a whole could endanger an investment's value. Environmental and tax legislation can have a dramatic impact on certain investment values, up or down. It is important to note this risk when investing.

Currency Risk: An investment in international securities can be affected by foreign exchange rate changes, political and economic instability, as well as differences in accounting standards.

Asset Protection Risk: Risk that is associated with a loss of net worth due to lawsuits, malpractice claims, etc. The higher your income and net worth is, the greater the risk. The more complex planning goes beyond the scope of this text and includes titling and ownership issues, legal documents, etc.

Diversity Risk: This will be discussed at length later in the book, but allow us to overstate the obvious: DIVERSIFY!

In summary, a properly structured financial plan will balance all of these variables so that you are diversified by asset class, risk levels, tax treatment, and time horizon.

4

The Security and Confidence Stage: Emergency Funds

This stage is divided into three main sections with an emphasis on building up emergency reserves, making sure debt is under control, and taking care of risk management (insurance) needs. Each of these factors is equally important. Most people agree on the need to have money accessible for emergencies, to pay their debts, and to be adequately insured. The trick to the individual financial plan is to figure out the appropriate level for each of these.

1. Emergency Reserves

The one constant in life is that there will always be surprises. The purpose of an emergency reserve fund is just what it sounds like—money that is very accessible when you really need it. The main characteristic of an investment in this category would be the money that is liquid, yet safely invested, so the principal remains intact. The most common mistake people make here is not having adequate reserves or taking undue risk with these funds. This money needs to remain liquid in case of unexpected expenses, like car expenses, home repairs, job loss, or medical emergencies. For most people, peace of mind is the main benefit of having an adequate emergency reserve fund. When you are financially prepared for these surprises, they become less stressful and are therefore easier to deal with emotionally.

As a general rule of thumb, your emergency reserve account would be able to cover approximately three months of bills. So, if your monthly expenses are averaging

$7,000, then your emergency reserve fund should be $21,000. During your residency or fellowship, your expenses may be closer to $2,000 to $4,000 per month, depending on if you are married or single. Ideally, an emergency fund for a single resident would be around $6,000, and for a married couple possibly as high as $12,000. We realize this can be difficult to accumulate given your limited income. This is a rough guide, and you may want to consider having a higher emergency reserve if you anticipate a big purchase, such as a car or home. Ideally, you do not want to deplete your emergency reserve completely in order to purchase such items.

If you are self-employed in your own practice, it is also important to maintain a cushion in your business accounts in the event of an unexpected large expense or your inability to work for a period of time. Business overhead coverage does not begin paying for thirty to sixty days. So keeping two months of your overhead in reserves for your practice is recommended. Until you are able to accumulate this, have a line of credit approved and available to you in order to address short-term cash flow fluctuations.

The typical investments that can be used to hold your emergency reserves would include bank investments or money market funds. The common theme among these investments is their liquidity and the safety of the principal. If you use a bank for your emergency reserves, typically these funds are in savings accounts and interest-bearing checking accounts, as well as money market funds.

For safety of principal and liquidity, savings accounts are the most common option, but not necessarily the best. Such accounts are insured, so there is no market risk but lots of purchasing power risk. However, this also means there is typically a lower yield than other investments.

Another option is a CD (certificate of deposit) with a relatively short maturity. The disadvantage to a CD is that the money is tied up for a certain length of time, and removing the funds sooner will result in an interest rate penalty. To avoid this problem, it can make sense to stagger your CD maturities so that you always have some that come due every six months or so. Therefore, you can access it if you need to or reinvest it if you don't.

A money market mutual fund is often the best choice as an emergency reserve possibility. Many people incorrectly associate the term mutual fund with high risk. However, a mutual fund only has as much risk as the underlying investments it owns. A money market mutual fund pools investors' dollars in the typical mutual fund style, and purchases jumbo CDs through banks, treasury securities (T bills), as well as commercial paper. Most money market funds have a check writing privilege, which allows you to write checks against your account, subject to minimums of usually $250 or $500. The rate of return earned on these funds will fluctuate based on the short-term money market, but is typically competitive with the interest rate at the time. Investments in a money market fund are neither insured nor guaranteed by the FDIC, or any other government agency. Although the fund seeks to preserve the value of your investment at $1.00 per share, it is possible to lose money by investing in the fund.

A home equity line of credit is another excellent option. If you have equity in your house, and if interest rates are low and tax deductible, this option should not be discounted. In fact, in periods of time when there is a low interest rate environment, maintaining an open line of credit against your house equity is a favorable form of a source of emergency reserve cash. It could also be used to pay down a high-interest credit card or for a major purchase, like a car. The drawback is that it needs to be paid off when you sell your house, which of course would result in fewer proceeds at closing.

Life insurance cash values on permanent policies are another source of emergency funds. The returns vary, depending on the type of policy, so work carefully with your advisor to select a policy that fits your objectives. It is usually possible to take out a loan or borrow against your cash value, using it as collateral. Sometimes, you can take an outright withdrawal of the money. Remember, though, that any loans or withdrawals taken will reduce both the cash value and death benefit.

5

Debt Management

If you are in the fortunate situation of having no debts, congratulations! If you come from the school of thought that you don't ever want to owe anything to anybody, debt management is not an issue. However, in today's society, this ideology is very uncommon, and many people could use some strategies on effectively managing their debt.

The typical young physician has $80,000 to $200,000 in student loans. In addition, many have a car loan, personal loans, and credit card debt. Make it a priority to pay off all the higher-rate loans (currently those above 8 percent). As of the writing of this book, current federal student loan rates are around 4.7 percent, which makes student loans different. To lock in your low student loan rate, you need to consolidate prior to July 1. Once you have consolidated, your interest rate will be locked for the next thirty years if your balance exceeds $60,000. Most consolidation programs offer rate reductions for automating your payment, and for successive on-time payments. The interest rate charged on new and non-consolidated federal student loans changes each year on July 1.

You can make additional payments to your student loans without penalty to accelerate your debt reduction goals. So, the main motivation to reduce a 3 to 5 percent student loan is the good feeling of moving toward becoming debt-free. Your net worth, however, can grow faster by paying off higher-interest debt and/or investing at an after-tax rate of greater than the interest rate on your student loans. If rates climb to the cap of 8.25 percent for non-consolidated loans, it will most likely make sense at that point to aggressively pay off the debt.

Rates will most likely rise in the future, for new federal loans and non-consolidated loans. Deciding whether to consolidate or not as rates climb could be a difficult decision. You can only consolidate your loans one time. If you consolidated your loans in the late 1990s, you locked in to a much higher rate than today's. Unfortunately, you cannot reconsolidate to take advantage of the rates available now, so a good option may be to apply extra principal payments.

Student Loan Management During Residency or Fellowship

When you graduate from medical school, you will receive a six-month grace period on your federal student loans. After six months, you will either need to begin making payments, or file for economic hardship deferment or forbearance. If you have low loan balances, beginning payments can be a viable option. If you have federal student loan balances in excess of roughly $115,000, you should qualify for economic hardship deferment. Qualification is based on a formula set by the federal government. If you qualify, the federal government will continue to pay the interest on your subsidized loans. Your unsubsidized loans will accrue interest. You can qualify for economic hardship deferment for up to three years.

If you are not able to make payments and do not qualify for economic hardship deferment, you still have the option of filing for forbearance. Forbearance does not adversely affect your credit, and must be granted on federal loans during residency or fellowship. While in forbearance, you make no payments, but your subsidized and unsubsidized loans accrue interest. With current rates being so low, the cost to have $100,000 of student loans in forbearance is about $3,000 in interest per year, depending on when you consolidated. This is only about $1,500 more per year than deferment. This example assumes you had $50,000 of subsidized and $50,000 of unsubsidized loans.

Make sure when you finish a residency and enter a fellowship to clarify your employment status. Many programs consider fellows to be students. If this is the case, you can apply for true deferment again, just like when you were in medical school. To verify this, you will generally need to send a letter to your loan administration company from your program coordinator on the institution's letterhead attesting to your status.

If you have personal debt such as credit cards or high-interest personal loans, you should pay those off quickly, especially if the interest rate is above 10 percent. As each loan is paid off, apply the payment to another loan to accelerate your debt reduction. When all high-interest (greater than 10 percent) loans are paid off, it would be appropriate to begin contributions to 401(k)s, 403(b)s, IRAs, and other investments. If you have debt with an interest rate of 5 percent or lower, you can start saving for other financial goals and making minimum payments on the low-interest debts.

With mortgage debt and business debt, a similar analysis should be applied. However, mortgage and business debt have the additional advantage of being tax-deductible. Student loans are only deductible if you make less than $60,000 as a single taxpayer and $100,000 if you are married. The interest rate to use is the "after-tax" rate. For instance, a 6 percent mortgage for someone in a 30 percent tax bracket has an after-tax rate of 4.2 percent (6 percent x .7).

When purchasing a home, try not to finance more than two and a half to three times your annual income if you want to be financially independent at an early age. It can be difficult to stay within those parameters during your training. It is acceptable to buy a home that is a larger multiple of your income during this stage. This will allow you to get into the real estate market. The size house you buy when you enter practice should be under three times your annual income if you want to retire early. It is also advantageous to minimize the number of real estate transactions you engage in, because they involve substantial fees, commissions, and transaction costs.

You should also avoid private mortgage insurance, if possible. That can be done with a combination of two loans. One is a traditional mortgage, and the other is held by a bank as a home equity line of credit. Also, consider how long you plan on staying in a home when determining the best financing. If you plan to be in a home for only five years, you should choose a 5/1 ARM (adjustable rate mortgage) versus a fixed thirty-year loan. The interest rate will be lower on the 5/1 ARM, since the lender is only guaranteeing your rate for five years as opposed to thirty, even though both loans are amortized over thirty years.

Interest-only loans are also becoming more popular. During residency or fellowship, using an interest-only loan can allow you to buy a house you might not have been able to afford otherwise. If you choose an interest-only loan on a house once you are in practice, make sure you have a plan for the difference between the interest-only payment and the fixed thirty-year payment. Do not spend this money. For example, if your interest-only payment is $2,500 and your fixed thirty-year payment would be $3,000 per month, make sure you automatically save the $500 into an account that will earn at least as much as the interest rate. Using an interest-only loan allows you to maximize your home interest tax deduction each year, but will build equity only if the home appreciates.

The type of loan you use for your home can also be a function of the asset protection laws of your state. If your state protects the equity in your home from lawsuits, you may want to pay it off in a relatively short period of time and view it as conservative investment. If your state protects very little equity, you may want to use an interest-only loan and direct what would be the principal payment into a protected asset.

In this book, we are discussing issues from a financial perspective, and we realize that there is an emotional aspect to debt as well. Sometimes, the emotional dislike and stress of debt can outweigh the benefits of carrying very low-interest debt. In these situations, by all means, pay the loans off and free up your cash flow.

General Debt Guidelines and Information

- Prioritize your debt based on interest rates and eliminate the loans from the highest to the lowest rate.
- Pay off all debt with rates above 10 percent as soon as possible.
- Once you enter practice, do not finance more than 2.5 times your annual gross income on your home, if you want to be financially independent at an early age.
- Consolidate your student loans.
- Key date: July 1. This is the day rates change on variable federal student loans.
- There is also a new Web site at www.annualcreditreport.com that advertises that you can get a free credit report every year.

Check your credit report. It's a good idea to review your credit report every year. The financial information included in this report will have a bearing on whether you can obtain a loan, auto or home insurance, rent an apartment, or even apply for a job. Contact the credit bureaus and correct any errors you find.

6

Risk Management, Insurance, and Asset Protection

Protecting yourself against unforeseen catastrophic losses is the third critical area of the base of the pyramid and the *Security and Confidence Stage*. In fact, think of this as a three-legged stool. Kick one leg out, and the stool will not stand. The financial pyramid is just like that.

Important insurance coverage includes health, auto, disability, life, liability, malpractice, business overhead, disability buyout, long-term care, and homeowner's or renter's. In many cases, life and/or disability insurance are overlooked. However, these can be critically important, depending on your personal situation.

The reason for placing risk management at this point is obvious. You need to protect yourself from losses that would create such a hole that you may otherwise never dig yourself out of. Then, once you are on your way to financial independence, insurance plays an equally important role in protecting your assets.

While you don't want to have any gaps in your insurance protection, you certainly don't want to overlap or duplicate coverage. The ideal financial plan will have you paying reasonable premium levels while providing maximum protection. Remember, the major role of insurance is to protect against catastrophic losses. A common mistake is trying to insure too many contingencies or not using deductibles to your advantage.

You will want to ask yourself a couple of questions before purchasing insurance:

- Is the premium for this coverage going to dramatically affect my lifestyle?
- If I do not buy this coverage and suffer the losses that would have been covered, would I be in grave financial trouble?

If the answer to the first question is *no* and the answer to the second is *yes*, the insurance in question is right for you. If not, reconsider the structure and price of the insurance. Consult an experienced financial professional to help you determine the appropriate levels of coverage and how to structure your insurance within the context of a comprehensive financial plan.

When it comes to life insurance, it is easy to become confused. Some complicated terminology like "term life," "whole life," "universal life," "variable adjustable life," and so on, may put you off, but by understanding just a few terms and some of the benefits and disadvantages, you will be much better prepared to evaluate the coverage that is best for you. If structured correctly, life insurance can be one of the most versatile and powerful financial tools available, and should not be overlooked.

Life Insurance

Life insurance has many uses. The simplest need to understand is the need to protect the ones you care about in the event of your untimely death. Additional uses are to:

- Protect your family's financial security
- Secure a loan to buy a practice
- Accumulate and protect wealth (permanent life policies only)
- Pay estate taxes
- Draw more income from your retirement assets without the fear of leaving nothing to your heirs

- Provide liquid dollars in the event of an untimely death of a business partner
- Provide the insured person with peace of mind

Focusing on the simplest need for coverage, which is to protect the ones you care about in the event of your untimely death, it is important to understand how the policy works. Life insurance benefits are stated in a specific lump sum. For example, a $1,000,000 policy would pay $1,000,000 tax-free to the stated beneficiary upon death of the insured.

Since your income terminates at your death, it would be advisable to provide for a lump sum that would continue an adequate portion of your income to your family. For example, if you make $200,000 annually, and you die tomorrow and want to continue your $200,000 income indefinitely to your family, you will need about $4 million in life insurance. The $4,000,000 would be payable tax-free to your family. If the lump sum is invested at 5 percent interest, your family could draw $200,000 per year of taxable income without depleting the principal. It is wise to use a conservative investment return on death benefit proceeds, as beneficiaries will most likely be very conservative with managing the insurance money. This simple analysis does not factor in potential social security benefits or the long-term effects of inflation.

Life insurance is one of the only insurance coverages that people generally don't think about insuring to full replacement value. If your $500,000 home burned down, would you want it replaced with a $200,000 home? No. If your $200,000 income is lost to your family, do you want to replace it with a $50,000 income, $100,000 income, or full replacement of $200,000? Generally, most people would want to insure for full replacement value. The amount of life insurance you should own is the amount you would buy today if you knew you were going to die tomorrow.

Types of Life Insurance

There are two broad types of life insurance—term and permanent. To understand the difference, it is helpful to compare term insurance to renting an apartment and permanent life insurance to owning a home. Term insurance is inexpensive when you are young, but the cost increases exponentially as you age. You can buy a term policy where the premium goes up every year or stays level for five, ten, twenty, or thirty years. Term insurance provides a large amount of temporary coverage at a low cost for young, healthy people.

The cost for $1,000,000 of term insurance for a twenty-five- to thirty-five-year-old is between $25 and $50 per month, so protecting you and your family is quite affordable. Your term policy should be convertible to a permanent policy without medical underwriting. This guarantees that if your health changes, you do not need to worry about re-qualifying for the coverage after the initial term. So, be sure the company you purchase your term insurance with has a competitive permanent policy.

As a long-term strategy, some advisors recommend buying term insurance and taking the difference in premiums between the term and permanent policy and investing it. This can be an effective strategy if you have the discipline to invest the difference on a monthly basis, and are sure you will not want life insurance later in life. Keep in mind that over the course of twenty or more years, the tax implications of this strategy can become significant. The tax inefficiencies increase as you near retirement.

These inefficiencies are magnified when you reallocate your portfolio to become more conservative as you get older. This requires owning more bonds. To accomplish this, you must pay capital gains taxes when you sell your stock portfolio to buy bonds. Bonds also generate ordinary income, which for highly compensated physicians will be at a higher tax rate than the capital gain and dividend distributions from your stock portfolio. Taxes are owed annually on this strategy, because most physicians will have exhausted their tax-deferred investment options such as 401(k)s, IRAs, SEPs, or profit-sharing plans. This leaves only taxable accounts to invest the difference in premiums between the term and permanent policy.

Permanent life policies have a fixed premium where a portion of the premium is allocated to a tax-deferred account called the cash value, and a portion is allocated to the cost of the policy. This is similar to a mortgage payment where some of your payment pays interest and some principal. The cash either pays a fixed percentage or allows you to direct your money to a wide range of conservative to aggressive sub-accounts. For many people, permanent life policies are too expensive. However, physicians often have higher incomes, placing them in a high tax bracket. So a permanent life policy can be a very appropriate long-term product to diversify a financial plan. This is especially true if you meet the following criteria:

- You have a need for life insurance
- Your income is too high to qualify for a Roth IRA contribution, or you are phased out of the Roth IRA
- You are funding your current qualified plan at the maximum level
- You will have a significant net worth now or at retirement
- You have additional discretionary dollars that can be used for long-term financial security
- You are looking for additional ways to defer investment income from tax
- You want to be able to spend more of your other retirement assets without the fear of leaving nothing to your heirs

A sound strategy is to fund a policy right at or just under the modified endowment (MEC) limits. This maximizes the accumulation portion compared to the insurance expenses.

There are many types of permanent life insurance. It is advisable to make sure the kind you are considering is designed for your intended use, whether it be family protection, estate planning, business continuation, or supplemental retirement income. As of the writing of this book, states such as Florida, Texas, Kansas, New York, and Tennessee also protect 100 percent of the policies' cash value or equity in the event of a judgment against you. Other states provide partial protection. Depending on your level of concern, this issue should also be considered when determining how to structure your life insurance.

This is one of the most complex financial products in the marketplace, so be sure you work with a competent, knowledgeable, and experienced advisor.

Disability Insurance

When you break down a financial plan and the desire to become financially independent, your income and savings level will determine your success. If your ability to earn an income is interrupted, the plan will fall apart quickly unless you protect yourself.

The odds of a long-term disability (lasting ninety days or longer) are six to seven times greater than a death during your working years. Financially, a long-term disability is worse than death, because your expenses rise and you are still around. Early in your career, the only way to guarantee your income will not stop if something happens to your ability to earn an income is to insure yourself with a quality occupation-specific disability insurance policy. By occupation-specific, this means if you cannot perform the duties of your specialty, you will be compensated. Other important features to make sure you include in your policy are the following:

- **Future Purchase Option:** This option allows you to add coverage to your policy in the future without medical underwriting. With disability insurance being quite difficult to obtain due to stringent underwriting, this is particularly important. The following are some examples of issues that can make it difficult to obtain or increase a personal policy:
  - History of mental/nervous/stress counseling
  - Diabetes
  - Excessive speeding tickets/DWI
  - Back pain, chiropractic concerns
  - Elevated liver enzymes
  - Abnormal weight
- **Guaranteed Renewal/Non-Cancelable Policy:** Once the policy has been issued, the company cannot change your rate or cancel the policy.

> It is a unilateral contract, meaning only you can make a change to the policy.

- **Inflation Protection**: This option makes sure that if you file a claim, the monthly benefit will increase with inflation. Over twenty-five years, at only 3 percent inflation, a $200,000 income will need to grow to $418,000 to have the same purchasing power, and that increase needs to be protected.

- **HIV Positive Protection**: If your specialty puts you at a higher risk for HIV, you will want to make sure your policy recognizes HIV as a disability. Many do not!

- **Residual Disability Benefit**: This option ensures that if your injury or illness limits your ability to practice only partially, the policy will pay a partial or proportionate benefit. Without this option, the policy only pays if you are totally disabled from your occupation.

Disability insurance is not an exciting area of planning, but until you have accumulated enough money to retire, it is one of the most important fundamental financial considerations. A disability policy will keep your financial life in order in the event of a disability, but should not significantly impact your ability to save for the future.

We are now seeing a trend where medical schools are providing group policies to protect their students in the event of disability. These policies provide a reduced amount of coverage for the first- and second-year students, and a larger benefit for the third- and fourth-year students. Some of these policies also offer up to $150,000 of student loan repayment in the event of permanent disability.

It is also typical for many large group practices to provide disability coverage for you. These policies typically will cover about 60 percent of your income. If the practice pays the premium for you and deducts the cost as a business expense, the benefit paid by the insurance company to you in the event of a claim will be considered taxable income.

If the group policy is not portable, or you would like more of your income protected than 60 percent, then you should obtain an individual policy.

Remember, you get what you pay for. Searching the Internet for the cheapest insurance policy often results in coverage that will not protect you and your family adequately. A competent insurance agent or financial planner can provide a valuable service and should be used. They can be the best resource in helping you maximize your coverage at appropriate prices. At claim time, they can help you with the paperwork. Choosing someone you trust, especially someone who comes recommended from a reliable source, will prove invaluable.

Umbrella Liability Coverage and Asset Protection

As your assets grow, it is wise to expand your umbrella liability insurance coverage. The limits built into most homeowner and auto policies are minimal. This coverage actually protects you and your assets in the event you or a family member cause harm due to your negligence. You are also protected in the event of negligence on your property. During residency, you should maintain at least $1 million in umbrella coverage. Once in practice, $2 to $5 million is recommended. The cost is normally around $100 to 150 per million of coverage per year. In addition, be sure to ask your agent for excess umbrella liability coverage for uninsured or underinsured motorists. This coverage protects you and your family for negligent acts caused by others.

You should also review your overall financial plan to see what assets are at risk in the event of a lawsuit. Unfortunately, we live in a society where successful or wealthy people are targeted for lawsuits more than other groups. As a physician and business owner, you are also subject to risk.

Each state has different laws in regards to protected assets. Some examples of assets that are protected in certain states are your personal residence, cash value life insurance, annuities, or a car. Your qualified plans such as 401(k)s, 403(b)s, SEPs, and profit-sharing plans are protected at the federal level. You should talk with your advisor to see how your state views various assets. You can lower your risk by insuring properly, incorporating your practice, and drafting appropriate legal documents. Again, work with a specialist who knows the asset protection laws of your state.

In states that grant extensive statutory protections, your asset protection plan is simpler than in states granted few protections. You can simply direct your money to the protected places such as IRAs, annuities, qualified plans, cash value life insurance, and your home. If your state has few statutory protections or you are investing in a non-protected asset in a state with good protections, you need to be more creative. One of the first things you can do is not own anything personally. This can be done by utilizing a family limited partnership (FLP) or limited liability company (LLC). Once an asset is owned inside the FLP or LLC, it becomes better protected in the event of a judgment against you.

For example, if a judgment is successful against you, the suing party can attach to your LLC. This means that when you do finally take money out, they will get paid then. The catch is that once they attach, they are responsible for the taxes on their respective share of what they are owed. So, if the judgment was for $1,000,000 and your assets in the LLC earned 4 percent, you would send the suing party a K1 for $40,000 at the end of the year. So, it would cost them $10,000 to $17,000 per year in taxes to wait. Most people will not attach to an LLC or FLP for that reason.

You can also get into more complex planning via the use of asset-protected trusts to own your LLC or FLP. At net worths in the multi-millions, some people also look to offshore accounts. If you have an LLC in an offshore account, you have great protections, since United States judgments are not valid in foreign countries. The cost to establish offshore accounts and have the money managed can be quite expensive. Keep in mind, having money offshore does not mean you do not pay taxes on it. The income liability is still the same, no matter what country your money is in.

There are additional methods of protecting your investments, your home equity, and your accounts receivable. This complex and important planning is discussed in an excellent text, <u>Wealth Protection, M.D.</u> by Jarvis and Mandell.

Business Continuation Planning

The focus of this section is to discuss the basics of structuring a business continuation plan for your private practice. This is a very detailed topic, and we will address the main issues. We are assuming everyone has made arrangements for their business liability, property, and equipment, and we will focus on the less understood risk management issues. With any small business, the untimely passing, disability, retirement, or termination of an owner or partner can present significant financial challenges.

When you buy in or become a partner, you will normally adopt and sign a shareholder agreement. In the agreement, the partners will typically specify what will happen in the event of a death, disability, or termination of one of the partners. Normally, the partners will mutually agree to buy out the deceased, disabled, or departing partner's interest for a specified value based on a formula. It is important to update your valuation periodically.

Without a well-designed strategy, there can be conflicts between the remaining owners and departed owners or heirs relating to distribution of income and the sale of the business. It may also be difficult for the remaining owner(s) to quickly come up with the funds to buy out the departed owner's interest. A well-designed business continuation plan will provide funding for the deceased, disabled, terminated, or retired partner's shares in the practice. This can be done through the use of life insurance, savings, or disability buyout coverage.

In the event of death or disability in a professional corporation, it is very important to have this structured properly due to the limitations that limit stock ownership to licensed practitioners only. The best way to guarantee that money will be available is to have life insurance and disability buyout insurance in place on all the partners sufficient to cover the buyout.

In the event of death, the most common types of arrangements are the stock redemption and cross purchase strategies. The following briefly summarizes each option.

Stock Redemption

- The corporation is the owner and beneficiary of the life insurance
- The cost of the policies is spread among the shareholders
- If you are using permanent life policies, the cash values are subject to corporate creditors
- Only one policy per shareholder is required (this is advantageous for large groups)
- The death benefit may be subject to the alternative minimum tax

Cross Purchase

- Shareholders own and are the beneficiaries of the life insurance policies on their partners
- The cost of insurance is higher for younger shareholders that pay for policies on the older partners
- Cash values are subject to the shareholders' creditors in most states if you are using permanent policies
- The death benefit is not subject to the alternative minimum tax

For larger groups, it is common to use the stock redemption strategy, and in practices with three or fewer owners, a cross purchase plan can work well.

Business Overhead Expense Coverage

If you are unable to work for an extended period of time, the results on your practice can be devastating. You should review your situation to see if your practice could withstand the loss of revenue you or your partners generate. If the loss of the revenue would result in financial difficulty, it is advisable to purchase a business overhead expense policy. These policies pay the overhead of your practice if you or a partner is disabled. Most policies begin to pay in thirty, sixty, or ninety days, and pay for twelve to twenty-four months. The goal is to keep your practice viable financially, so you can resume working when you recover from your disability.

According to the Health Insurance Association of America, 30 percent of all people age thirty-five to sixty-five will suffer a disability for at least ninety days, and about one in seven can expect to become disabled for five years or more. The average duration of a disability lasting more than ninety days, beginning prior to age sixty-five, is four years, and four months for ages forty to forty-four, four years and seven months for ages forty-five to forty-nine, and four years and six months for ages fifty to fifty-four.

Make sure the policy will pay if you cannot perform the material duties of your specialty. A policy that pays if you cannot do any occupation is not acceptable for a physician.

Expenses normally considered as business expenses would include the following:

- Compensation and employer-paid benefits
- Salary of a non-family member hired to replace you
- Rent and lease payments
- Utility costs
- Maintenance and service
- Legal and accounting fees
- Property and liability insurance
- Malpractice and business insurance
- Professional dues
- Business debt and interest
- Business property taxes
- Supplies
- Postage

If you are starting a practice or expect your practice to grow, you should add a future increase option to your policy. This option allows you to add more coverage to your policy without having to answer any medical questions. The increase is subject to financial review only.

Disability overhead expense policies are deductible as a business expense. Most policies have a waiting period of thirty, sixty, or ninety days, with the shorter waiting period being more expensive. The policy should be for the amount of overhead you are responsible for. Some insurance companies will limit the amount of coverage you can apply for to $25,000 per month.

You should also select a benefit period that matches your situation. The benefit period sets the number of months the policy will pay. The most common benefit periods are twelve, eighteen, or twenty-four months. You can also add additional options to the policy, such as the residual disability rider. This option assures that the policy will pay if you are partially disabled but still able to perform limited duties.

Disability Buyout Insurance

A disability buyout policy will provide a lump sum to your business partner(s) or the practice in the event of a long-term disability to you or your partner(s). This will ensure that the disabled partner receives a timely buyout, and it provides the necessary liquidity to the practice to buy out the disabled partner. Many practices insure the buyout at death of a partner, but do not consider the impact of a partner that is disabled and can no longer practice or generate revenue. Financially, the impact is just as significant. Statistically, a thirty-five-to fifty-five-year-old male is almost twice as likely to become disabled than die, and a female age thirty-five to fifty-five is nearly three times as likely to become disabled.

As the group grows in size, the odds of a disability among partners increases. The size of the assets to buffer the shock to the group should also grow. See the chart below showing the probability of at least one long-term disability prior to age sixty-five.

Number of Owners

Age	2 lives	3 lives	4 lives	5 lives	6 lives
25	36.5%	49.4%	59.7%	67.8%	74.4%
35	34.2%	46.7%	56.7%	64.9%	71.5%
45	31.1%	42.8%	52.5%	60.6%	67.3%
55	23.4%	33%	41.4%	48.7%	55.1%

As the group grows to ten or more, the odds are over 90 percent that one partner will be disabled for ninety days or longer. (Source: 1985 Society of Actuaries DSP Experience Tables.)

Buyout policies have a waiting period that requires the disability to last a specified period of time before paying the lump sum. The most common waiting periods are one year, eighteen months, or two years. The waiting period also prevents a buyout from occurring too soon. It should be fairly clear after eighteen months if the disabled partner is recovering, and whether the buyout should happen.

If you or your partner(s) work until a normal retirement age, you should also address other issues, such as:

- How will the practice buy out the retiring partners?
- What will the retiring partner do in regard to life and health insurance?
- How will the tail malpractice coverage be handled?

A well-designed business continuation plan will help facilitate and fund the sale of your practice in the event of a premature death or disability, and in the event of a long, healthy life.

In many cases, insurance is thought of as a "necessary evil." You have to have it, but it only benefits you if you have a claim. We look at insurance coverage as a valuable part of an overall comprehensive financial plan. The peace of mind you have by knowing you and your family are covered is worth a lot. In addition, you can be more aggressive with your other savings and investments, because you know your risk management needs are taken care of.

Looking back to the Middle Ages, we get a glimpse of the importance of insurance. People of wealth built fabulous castles and filled them with treasures. They always devoted significant resources to protecting those assets in the form of an army, a moat, and so on. In a sense, that was an early form of an insurance policy. So, as you continue to build your net worth, you should review and update your insurance to be sure you are maximizing your coverage and protecting you and your family, and your wealth.

7

The Capital Accumulation Stage

This stage represents a large amount of assets you will build up over your lifetime. The assets that tend to comprise this stage are quite varied. Some of the investments include individual stocks and bonds, mutual funds, variable life insurance cash values, and equity in real estate or your practice. Aside from the equity you build into your retirement plan, the majority of your financial independence will come from these investments. While these assets can also serve as emergency reserves, the investment horizon is usually five years or longer.

Keep in mind that all investments have risk. However, there are varying degrees and types of risk. The risk most often associated with an investment involves a fluctuating principal or a sudden depreciation in the stock market, as in October of 1987 or the bear market of 2000 to 2002. A corporate bond or government security holds the risk of loss of principal due to an increase in interest rates. Even a safe investment in a money market fund has purchasing power risk, because after taxes and inflation are figured in, your dollars could be worth less than when you originally invested. A summary of the types of risk is found towards the end of Chapter Three.

Saving money is one of the most important criteria in assuring financial success. As your income increases, get in the habit of allocating at least 20 percent of your gross income to debt reduction and/or investments. By living below your total income, your net worth will grow substantially, and you will cultivate a responsible attitude toward your money. Keeping up with the Jones' has become a national epidemic, but the real truth is that the millionaires next door don't concern themselves with flaunting their wealth, which explains why they are wealthy.

Generally speaking, real estate has long been a favorite investment tool for its tax benefits and as a buffer against inflation. Although there can be significant investment benefits in the long term, buying real estate is not without its risks. Deflation may decrease property values, or suspected long-term growth in a given area may not occur. Changes in tax law may reduce or eliminate anticipated tax benefits. Also, real estate is not liquid, so the necessity of a quick sale may require a substantial reduction in price.

The term "stock" or "share" both refer to a partial ownership interest in a corporation or equity. As a stockholder, you'll be able to vote for the company's board of directors and receive information on the firm's activities and business results. You may share in "dividends" or current profits.

Investors typically buy and hold stock for its long-term growth potential. Stocks with a history of regular dividends are often held for both income and growth. As the long-term growth of a company cannot be predicted, the short-term market value of the company's stock will fluctuate. If your financial need or your fear causes you to sell when the market is "down" (also called a "bear market"), a capital loss can result. If the market is "up" (also called a "bull market"), the investor can realize a capital gain when selling.

While stocks represent ownership in a business, bonds are debt issued by institutions such as the federal government, corporations, and state and local governments. At the bonds' "maturity," the principal amount will be returned. In the meantime, bond holders receive interest. When first issued, a bond will have a specified interest rate, or "yield." If a bond is traded on a public exchange, the market price will fluctuate, generally with changes in interest rates.

Using a mutual fund is an excellent way to lower your risk, because you are diversifying through a number of stocks. A properly designed mutual fund portfolio is generally the most appropriate method of accumulating wealth at this point in the financial pyramid. Some funds have high "market risk," meaning they can fluctuate quite dramatically. Past experience shows funds that have the most risk have upside and downside potential that needs to be carefully considered. Funds with low market risk often have "inflation risk." These funds usually produce lower returns that may not keep up with inflation.

If your investment horizon is relatively short (up to five years), then a more conservatively balanced fund, equity income fund, or even a medium-term corporate bond or government securities fund, will likely be the most appropriate. When your investment horizon is longer, growth-oriented stock funds are generally going to be the best choice. Again, each circumstance is different, and the advice of a competent professional will be valuable. Most firms have a short investment attitude questionnaire that you can answer to help determine the appropriate asset allocation strategy that meets your needs.

Diversify! Diversify! Diversify! Nothing else will be as crucial to your portfolio as diversifying and having a long-term vision. It's important to diversify not only by asset class, but also by tax treatment and time horizon. We all know the proverb, "Don't put all your eggs in one basket." Well, take it to the extreme—don't put all the baskets on the same truck, and don't drive all the trucks down the same road. It's not necessary to look too far back to recall the faddish investing in technology and startup companies of the late 1990s. Too many investors lost too much when the overvalued stocks plunged, and those eager investors expecting big returns were left with substantial losses.

Sometimes misunderstood, the main goal of diversification is not to maximize your return, but to minimize your risk and lower your volatility. The basic premise is that there is as much risk in being out of the market when it goes up as being in the market when it goes down, especially for your long-term money. As an example, take the period between 1926 and

2004, a period of 924 months; if you were out of the market during the thirty top performing months—about 3.6 percent of the time—you would have ended up with a return similar to treasury bills. While diversification does not guarantee against loss, it is a method used to manage risk.

Some additional strategies to employ when investing include dollar cost averaging and portfolio rebalancing. Dollar cost averaging is the process of investing a fixed amount of money each month (or quarter, or year) without worrying about whether the market is up or down. When it is down, you will buy more shares, bringing your average share price down. Over time, besides the element of forced savings, you will hopefully see returns that you are happy with. Dollar cost averaging does not assure a profit, nor does it protect against loss in declining markets. This investment strategy requires regular investments, regardless of the fluctuating price of the investment. You should consider your financial ability to continue investing through periods of low price levels.

When there is a large amount of money to invest, coming up with an investment policy and adhering to it is a must. Once an overall asset allocation mix is chosen based on your goals and objectives, stick to it and change only if there are significant changes in the economy, the portfolio, and/or your goals and objectives. Then, on a regular basis, either quarterly, semiannually, or annually, rebalance the portfolio back to the asset allocation you had started with. With this strategy, your investment mix does not get skewed towards more or less risk and volatility. Many current portfolio managers have the capability of providing this rebalancing process on an automatic basis.

A well-balanced portfolio is properly diversified by the following asset decisions:

- Stocks, bonds, real estate equity, and cash
- United States (domestic) investment versus international securities
- Large cap versus small cap stocks
- Growth versus value stocks (keep this in balance!)

There are many good resources to turn to that will help you take this process much further than the scope of this book. We think some of the best information can come from a competent and qualified financial advisor who will listen to you and develop a plan that meets your needs.

In general, a higher investment risk is best for those who:

- can accept short-term losses;
- can buy shares during a down market;
- believe gains will offset losses over the long run;
- will not leave the investment if one or two bad years occur; and
- have a long "investment time horizon."

The best way to learn sound market advice is to listen to the experts. The following quotes from mutual fund leaders all stress the futility of market timing:

Peter Lynch: *"My single most important piece of investment advice is to ignore the short-term fluctuations of the market. From one year to the next, the stock market is a coin flip. It can go up or down. The real money in stocks is made in the third, fourth, and fifth year of your investments, because you are participating in a company's earnings, which grow over time."*

Warren Buffet: *"I do not have, never have had, and never will have an opinion where the stock market will be a year from now."*

Sir John Templeton: *"Ignore fluctuations. Do not try to outguess the stock market. Buy a quality portfolio and invest for the long term."*

So, to drive it home, *invest for the long term and be patient.*

8

The Tax-Advantaged Stage

The focus of this stage is to try and significantly delay, reduce, and/or minimize the impact of taxes on your financial picture. Why? To accumulate and create the highest net worth you possibly can. One method of delaying the tax involves investing dollars into qualified retirement plans. This means the dollars are made on a before tax (qualified) basis. Again, the taxes are not eliminated. They are just deferred until the funds are withdrawn. These plans include individual retirement accounts (IRAs), simplified employee pensions (SEPs), tax-sheltered annuities (TSAs), pension and profit-sharing plans, 401(k) plans, 403(b) plans, and so on. We will discuss qualified plans for practices later.

The main advantage behind these plans is that the government has given you a significant motivation to save money. This is because your taxable income is reduced dollar for dollar by the contribution, which will then save you 20 to 45 percent of the deposit in taxes, depending on your income. In other words, your adjusted gross income is less, which means your taxable income is reduced. If you have taken care of the security and confidence level of your plan, you should always contribute to the 401(k) or qualified plan up to where the employer matches those funds if you plan to be at your current job long enough to be vested. Ideally, funding your qualified plan to the maximum level is a great strategy to accumulate wealth and reduce your current taxes.

While these accounts are good places to defer and delay the tax liability during your working years, they present some problems at retirement.

Remember, you aren't eliminating the tax, you are deferring it. The general principal is to save money into these plans when you are in a higher tax bracket, and withdraw the funds at retirement when you are in a lower tax bracket. However, if you do a good job saving in these plans, you may not be in a lower tax bracket at retirement due to the large amounts of money you will be pulling out of the plan when you retire. Transferring qualified assets to heirs can also present some tax nightmares if not handled carefully. Currently, income and estate taxes, when combined at the death of the second spouse, can run higher than 75 percent on qualified plans.

This is why it is very important if you are going to accumulate significant wealth that you diversify not only your investments, but the taxation of your investments. If you have aspirations to pass on money to your children, a foundation, church, university, or any other entity, it is important to compliment qualified plans with assets that pass more efficiently. Examples of this can be a non-qualified asset like a stock or mutual fund that receives a stepped up basis at death or life insurance that will pass income tax-free. These assets will still be included for estate taxes if owned personally.

For the resident physician or fellow, qualified plans are normally not a great option unless they are matched. Assuming you will be in a higher tax bracket in retirement than in training, you would not want to deduct your contribution on the 25 percent bracket and pull it out at retirement and pay 40 percent tax. A Roth IRA would be a wiser choice at this stage, assuming you have adequate cash flow, and no high-interest rate debt.

The reason the Tax-Advantaged Stage belongs above the Capital Accumulation and Security and Confidence Stages of the pyramid is because the money deposited into these plans is normally not available until you reach the age of fifty-nine and a half. There are methods of getting your money out early (72t, borrowing, disability, financial hardship). However, money flowing into these plans should be regarded as retirement money that cannot be touched until then.

Calculating Your Tax Bracket

We have taken the 10,000-page tax code and narrowed it down to two pages (see pages 71 and 72). Wouldn't it be nice if preparing our taxes was that easy! This is, of course, a basic guide only, just for educational purposes, and it doesn't factor in some of the specifics such as child care, student loan interest deductions, moving expenses, and so on. But, surprisingly, this is fairly accurate in estimating your federal tax liability.

We encourage working with your accountant, running one of the tax software packages, or simply using this guide any time you have a major change in your life that will affect your taxes. Family changes such as a birth, death, or a marriage all affect the tax you owe. Financial changes such as a new job, a raise, going back to school, and buying or moving to a new house, will also impact your tax liability, and a new calculation should be made. Compare your calculation to the amount you are having withheld from your paycheck, and if you are withholding too much, change this with your employer by filling out a new W-4 form.

This is especially useful if you are graduating in May or June and starting employment mid-year. If you don't work with your employer on the correct tax withholding, they will take out an amount that would correspond to you working for the whole year. Generally, there are many expenses, and having a higher take-home pay would most likely be more beneficial than getting a tax refund the following spring.

There are some important basic points to understand about taxes. First, getting a large refund isn't really all that smart. It means you just gave the government an interest-free loan for the year. If you are a terrible saver and use this as a forced savings plan, we're guessing it still backfires on you because you know the lump sum tax refund is coming and you have plans for spending that amount, too! In any event, we suggest you estimate your tax liability in advance and try to end up about even. That avoids any under-withholding penalties, and also any unexpected tax liability due that you may not be prepared for.

The second point is that it is always in your best interest to make more money! We've heard people say, "I just got a raise (or a bonus, or whatever) and it jumped me into the next tax bracket, so I'm going to take home less!" That's not how it works. The tax system is a progressive tax, and the more income you make, the more you take home. It's just that each additional dollar is taxed at a higher percentage, but the first dollars are taxed the same. Repeated, moving into a higher tax bracket affects the last of the dollars you earn, but the first dollars are still taxed at the same rate.

As an example, let's look at the Basic Federal Tax Estimator on the next page. Plug in your income (wages, interest income, etc.) and subtract contributions to pretax accounts to get your adjusted gross income. From that, you subtract your personal exemptions and either the standard deduction or your itemized deductions, whichever is higher. Then, look up your tax bracket on the chart. The tax bracket is the tax on each additional dollar you earn, or the tax that is saved by virtue of reducing your taxable income by a dollar.

Suppose you are married and starting in a practice and your taxable income happens to be exactly $119,950. Your best friend's taxable income comes in at $119,951, or $1 more (just into the 28 percent tax bracket). Many people think this is bad situation. The reality is that their tax liability is only 28 cents more than yours, because each new dollar is taxed at the 28 percent rate. They still have a take-home pay of 72 cents more than you, so while at a higher tax bracket, their take-home pay is more. The total tax is calculated as follows:

First $14,600 of taxable income:	$1,460 ($14,600 x .1)
Next $44,800 of taxable income:	$6,720 ($44,800 x .15)
Next $60,550 of taxable income:	$15,137 ($40,399 x .25)
Total Tax:	$23,317

Your friend's tax bill would be calculated the same as yours with another 28 cents of tax liability on the $1 above $119,950 at the 28 percent tax bracket. Work through your own situation a few times, and this should be easier to understand.

Basic Federal Tax Estimator

(This is a guide only. This does not factor in child care, student loan interest deductions, medical expenses, moving, etc.)

Gross Income: *Wages, Interest Income, etc.*

$_____

Minus: **Adjustments:** *IRA, 401(k), TSA, etc.*

$_____

Equals: **Adjusted Gross Income (AGI)**

$_____

Minus:

$_____

Personal Exemptions ($3,200 x # in household)
(Phased out as income exceeds certain limits)

And the higher of:

Standard Deduction (Single - $5,000; Married - $10,000)

Or

Itemized Deductions

☐   State Income Tax

☐   Home Mortgage Interest and Property Tax

☐   Charitable Contributions

Equals: **Taxable Income**

$_____

Federal Income Tax Due: (See tax table on next page)

$_____

2005 Individual Income Tax Rates

Single				Married Filing Jointly			
$	- to	7,300	10.00%	$	- to	14,600	10.00%
7,301	to	29,700	15.00%	14,601	to	59,400	15.00%
29,701	to	71,950	25.00%	59,400	to	119,950	25.00%
71,951	to	150,150	28.00%	119,951	to	182,800	28.00%
150,151	to	326,450	33.00%	182,801	to	326,450	33.00%
326,451	-		35.00%	326,451	-		35.00%

Let's turn our attention to the topic of qualified (pretax) retirement plans that may be offered through your employer, or that you can set up if you are self-employed. If you are looking for additional ways to reduce your taxable income, the biggest tax deductions can come from qualified plans set up through your practice. A qualified plan will be appropriate if you want to reduce taxes, save for retirement, and/or reward and retain good employees. Qualified plan assets are also protected from creditors.

Some possible drawbacks of qualified plans as referenced earlier are:

- The money is generally not available without penalty until age fifty-nine and a half (although there are exceptions to this rule)
- All distributions are taxed as ordinary income when received
- Setup and annual administration fees can be high
- Upon death, the combined taxes can be over 75 percent for large balances when you add in the current income tax and estate taxes if the proceeds are paid to a non-spouse, non-charity beneficiary

Here is a brief discussion of the various retirement plans.

Simple IRAs

A Simple IRA is often the starting point for a physician who may be moonlighting in residency, contracting themselves to a hospital, or owning a small private practice. The setup fees and annual maintenance fees are minimal. A Simple IRA allows for any owner or employee to contribute up to $10,000 in 2005, pretax, as long as $10,000 does not exceed 100 percent of income. The employer must also choose a matching contribution of 1 to 3 percent per year or a flat 2 percent contribution for any eligible employees. For example, if the practice chose a 3 percent match and a employee making $30,000 contributes 3 percent of his or her income to the plan, the practice would need to contribute 3 percent as well, or $900. The practice would also make a matching contribution to the owner(s). The match is immediately vested. Vesting refers to a schedule that can be placed on certain retirement plans that requires employees to work for a specified period of time before the money contributed to the plan by the employer is theirs if they leave.

401(k) Plans

A 401(k) plan is similar to a Simple IRA plan, with main differences being contribution limits, vesting schedules, and fees. In 2005, you can defer up to $14,000 into a 401(k). If you had a 401(k) with a 3 percent match, assuming $160,000 income, the total funding could be $18,800 ($14,000 + [$160,000 x 3 percent] = $18,800). You can also have a vesting schedule on the matching contribution. This means matched contributions would not be available to employees if they left the practice within a certain time period. A normal vesting schedule is 20 percent in the first year grading to 100 percent in five years. 401(k) plans do require more monitoring than Simple IRAs. It is important to make sure your employees are contributing to a basic 401(k) plan, or your plan may be deemed top-heavy, which limits your contribution amount.

Safe Harbor 401(k) Plans

A Safe Harbor 401(k) cannot be deemed top-heavy. It functions like a traditional 401(k), except the practice is required to make a contribution of 3 percent of compensation for everyone eligible. This is not a match. It is a required contribution and is vested immediately. If the employer is willing to contribute 3 percent of eligible payroll, the top-heavy testing is not necessary, and the highly compensated owner can contribute the maximum amount each year.

Profit-Sharing Plans

Profit-sharing plans are qualified plans where employers can make discretionary contributions that may vary from year to year. Each employee receives the same contribution percentage, unless the plan is designed to take advantage of permitted disparity rules. Some of these permitted changes to contribution amounts for participants can be based on age or integrated with social security.

It is also possible to assign classes to employees. These permitted disparity rules allow owners to allocate a higher percentage of the dollars to the older or more highly compensated people in the practice. This will typically be the owners and associates. The contributions are usually based on business profits, but according to the IRS rules, you can also contribute to your plan based on compensation.

The maximum deductible contribution that can be made to a profit-sharing plan is 25 percent of eligible compensation, to a maximum of $42,000 in 2005. Eligible compensation is all the compensation an employer pays to eligible plan participants during the employer's tax year. Contributions are tax-deductible, and earnings accumulate on a tax-deferred basis. The employer takes the deduction for this contribution. The employer's contribution to each employee's account is not considered taxable income to the employees for the contribution year.

In very profitable practices or specialty clinics, it is common to see a profit-sharing plan together with a safe harbor 401(k). Together, the limit is still $42,000. This way, the owners can contribute the $14,000 throughout the year plus the 3 percent safe harbor contribution and determine at the end of year if they want to contribute the remaining balance to max out the plan at $42,000.

Simplified Employee Pensions (SEP IRAs)

A SEP IRA is very similar to a basic profit-sharing plan, and it is also a good choice for a moonlighting physician and/or locum tenants, or if you are contracting your services to a hospital or health care facility. The contribution limits are essentially the same. However, you are not allowed to put a vesting schedule on a SEP IRA. Once a contribution is made for an employee, the employer may not recoup any of the contribution if the employee terminates employment. You must include all employees that have worked in three of the last five years. You are permitted to allow more immediate access to the plan, but not more restrictive. SEPs can be a good choice if you are the only employee and your staff is limited.

If you are self-employed or a partner in a practice and have not reviewed your qualified plan in the last three years, it would be advisable to look at your options. There have been many changes to qualified plans with recent legislation, making these plans much more attractive. It is important to have a clear vision of what you want the plan to accomplish before reviewing things. An owner would consider these two main questions:

- Do you want the plan to maximize your contribution with the lowest required contribution for your staff?
  Or
- Do you want to fund the plan so it is a retirement plan for you and your employees? In this case, you fund their accounts heavily in addition to yours, and the plan provides a significant benefit to the owner and the employees.

For those who have an interest and your cash flow allows setting aside more than $42,000 per year pretax, there are additional options such as cash balance plans. These plans normally make sense only for very productive practices with owners over the age of forty-five, and a small number of young employees. If you are getting a late start in your planning, we would strongly suggest you look into these plans.

In summary, qualified plans are an integral part of your retirement, and there are many ways in which you can design a plan. It is important to make sure your advisor fully understands all the plan design options to create a plan that maximizes the benefits you want and minimizes negatives.

There are also substantial tax benefits with a variety of non-qualified investments. The term "non-qualified" means there is no immediate tax deduction when contributing to these accounts, but the tax benefits can be more beneficial over your lifetime. The following assets are generally part of the Capital Accumulation Stage, but we'll provide the discussion of the tax reduction strategy of each technique in this chapter.

Stocks: As stocks appreciate in value (for this discussion, we'll assume they appreciate!), there is no tax due on the appreciation until the stock is sold. Along the way, if any dividends are paid, the tax rate is less (15 percent for the highest tax bracket) than if it was the ordinary income tax rate. In addition, when the stock is sold, if held for over a year, the gain is taxed at the lower 15 percent capital gain rate. So, there is a benefit of tax deferral during the holding period and tax minimizing due to the gain being treated as a capital gain.

Roth IRAs: Assuming you have all of your Security and Confidence Stage issues taken care of, and your income is such that you can use Roth IRAs, we would recommend it. The Roth is a very attractive option during your training if you have the cash flow to fund it. You have the ability to pay taxes on your contribution at your lower residency or fellowship income tax bracket, pay no tax as the account grows (hopefully, it grows), and you can pull the entire balance out tax-free when you are potentially in a much higher tax bracket at retirement. Would you rather pay tax on the seeds going into the ground or the end-of-the-year harvest? The seeds, of course!

Growth in a Roth IRA may not be withdrawn until the later of reaching age fifty-nine and a half or maintaining your Roth IRA for a period of five years. Keep in mind that withdrawals of your investment growth prior to this are subject to a 10 percent early withdrawal penalty. Roth IRA limits are $4,000 in 2005 to 2007 and $5,000 in 2008 to 2010. To fully contribute to a Roth IRA, your adjusted gross income (AGI) needs to be less than $95,000 if you are single and $150,000 if you are married. You are able to do a reduced contribution up to $110,000 of AGI if single and $160,000 of AGI if married. In most cases, a young practicing physician will have an income that is too high to allow for a Roth IRA. But, if you have the cash flow and qualify during school, or your first year out, then by all means, set up a Roth IRA. Then when your income is too high to qualify, you can achieve some similar results by funding a permanent life insurance policy, as discussed in chapter six.

Real Estate: Real estate can be an excellent method of building wealth. Getting away from rent and into your first home is one obvious way. Another is leveraging the equity you have in your existing real estate into additional property. The growth is tax-deferred, and there are some favorable strategies available upon the sale and/or disposition. As for financing your house, contrary to popular belief, it can make sense to put little money down and stretch the mortgage out (and the tax deduction) in favor of freeing up cash flow for other goals and objectives. For a comprehensive discussion of this topic, we'd encourage you to pick up Doug Andrew's book, *Missed Fortune 101*.

Life Insurance: The benefits of a life insurance policy are much like those of the Roth IRA, with some additional features. As an accumulation tool, there is a cost for the insurance, so this is appropriate for someone who is younger and in good health and has a longer investment time horizon. The cash values grow tax-deferred and can be accessed tax-free, if structured properly. It is generally best to avoid having the policy become a modified endowment policy (MEC), and working with a very knowledgeable insurance or financial professional is a must.

Having a permanent life insurance policy can help you maximize your overall net worth in some other ways, too. You reduce your need for term insurance, which frees up cash. In fact, the most beneficial time to have a permanent life insurance policy in place is at retirement because of all of the advantages it provides. Briefly, you can be more aggressive in using and enjoying your other assets, because the life insurance essentially provides a "permission slip" to do so. You are also building an asset that can be passed on very efficiently to the next generation, and will provide immediate cash to pay taxes on your other assets. This is particularly important if your plan has large illiquid assets such as real estate that may need be sold by your heirs to cover the tax if not planned for properly. Work with your financial advisor to coordinate this with your overall financial plan.

State-Sponsored 529 College Plans: There are a number of methods of putting investments in your children's or grandchildren's name. If the funds are ultimately to help them with their future college education expenses, a 529 plan is the answer. Some states allow a state tax deduction on the contributions, and all of the plans grow tax-deferred. If the funds are withdrawn for tuition, room and board, and "qualifying" education needs, the funds can be withdrawn tax-free also. These funds can even be transferred between family members. For a lengthier discussion, as well as a link to your state-sponsored plan, go to www.savingforcollege.com. However, make sure your own financial security is assured and your financial pyramid is sound before aggressively putting money into your children's accounts.

Annuities: An annuity is marketed by an insurance company as their answer to other investments. There are numerous benefits of non-qualified annuities as another financial instrument. Namely, they grow tax-deferred, you can switch between the separate accounts in a variable annuity without tax implications, and there are some death benefit guarantees to protect the value for your heirs. Withdrawals from annuities prior to age fifty-nine and a half are subject to a 10 percent early withdrawal penalty, as well as potential deferred sales charges. You also will want to review the asset protection laws of your state to see if annuities are protected. They are in numerous states, thus increasing their attractiveness as an investment.

What Do You Do at Retirement?

Estimating your retirement needs is an important factor to consider at this stage of the pyramid. A financial planning rule of thumb is to assume you will live on 70 to 80 percent of your pre-retirement income, although more and more people are enjoying a retirement lifestyle that matches their working years. This figure should be based on the income you plan to be earning at retirement, not that which you're making today. To estimate this, look at your current expenses and subtract the expenses and savings that will not be needed at retirement, and add in extra expenses (travel, medical, etc.) that may be needed then. Consider the following:

- Will you still be paying a mortgage?
- Will you still have children in college?
- Do you anticipate hefty medical expenses for yourself or your spouse?
- Do you wish to travel extensively?
- Will your day-to-day living expenses be similar, or less, than what they are now?

It is important to understand how your life will change at retirement, and establish a retirement plan that will allow you to enjoy retirement and provide you with flexibility to deal with the changes.

9

The Speculation Stage

The Speculation Stage involves risking money you can afford to lose. Some people are never comfortable with this, and thus should not consider it. These people should simply build their financial pyramid wider. This stage can involve different things for different people. It might mean investing into a small business you're starting, or investing in a friend's business. It could be buying very speculative individual stocks or aggressive specialty mutual funds.

Subjecting your money where the principal has a high degree of volatility and risk has potentially high returns, but your money could also be lost completely. It is appropriate that this stage fits at the top of the pyramid, because if the money is lost, it won't be devastating to your overall financial plan.

A good rule of thumb when deciding how much to risk in a business opportunity or other aggressive venture is one year's worth of net worth growth. Never invest more than that! In a worst case scenario, if you lost the entire amount of your investment, you have basically lost one year's worth of financial progress. While not fun, it is not financially devastating. People get into trouble and can't recover financially when they take a lifetime's worth of savings and gamble with it.

As an example, let's say your net worth is $200,000, and conservatively projected a year from now, it will be $225,000. This growth could be from additional savings, reducing debts, and/or growth from your existing assets.

In any event, the $25,000 projected growth is the maximum amount that should be considered for a very speculative investment.

In the event that an opportunity has come along which requires more than this amount, do not be tempted to risk more. Consider lowering your investment, delaying the timing until your net worth has grown, or involving a financial partner. The following ideas are just a few examples of possibilities that exist:

- Buying individual stocks of new companies
- Buying stock in initial public offerings (IPOs)
- Buying stock on margin (be very careful!)
- Investing in a friend's or family member's new business
- Buying raw land and/or real estate for speculation
- Trading commodities (be careful here!)

In summary, no one has ever gotten into trouble financially by being too conservative for too long. Sure, there are some potential lost "opportunity costs," but you can get into a lot of financial trouble by being too aggressive with too much money. That's why the financial pyramid is such a useful tool to help organize and prioritize these decisions.

10

Contracts, Agreements, and Other Considerations

In this chapter, we will discuss some key points to understanding and clarifying associate contracts, and summarize some advantages and disadvantages for different types of practices. We strongly encourage all physicians to utilize an attorney who is familiar with medical employment contracts. You want to eliminate any surprises. A common way to create misunderstanding is to wait until you are concluding your training to start looking for a practice and then rush through the contract negotiation phase. To avoid this, we recommend that you begin looking for a practice at least six to twelve months prior to finishing. Here are some important contract points to understand:

Initial terms – The initial terms will define when you start working and the length of employment. Many initial contracts will be for one year. If you have an interest in buying into the practice or becoming a partner, make sure all of the details are laid out. Also, determine a date for the valuation of the practice to be established and how the valuation will be determined. A valuation will normally use a three-year production average in addition to market conditions and other factors. If these terms are not discussed and put in the initial contract, the buy-in can be delayed, or worse yet, the whole practice can be broken apart.

Initial salary guarantee – A guarantee is normally stated as a base monthly or annual income. This can vary widely, depending on your specialty. You will likely have a production component to your income as well. This is based on your productivity, and is over and above your base salary. The production is normally paid as a bonus monthly, quarterly, semiannually, or annually. The sooner this is paid, the sooner you can get it working for you. Learn and understand the production formula so you how everything affects the bottom line.

Non-compete clauses or restrictive covenants – A non-compete clause or restrictive covenant is normal. It is designed to protect the hospital or practice you are joining from you leaving and creating a competitor in the area. They generally do not permit you to set up a new practice within a certain radius of the current practice for a specified length of time. The distance varies based on population density. If you are in a large city, the distance might be four to six miles. If you are practicing in a rural area, the distance could be over twenty-five miles. Be sure you understand all the details. If you work at a practice with multiple locations, occasionally the restrictive covenant will pertain to all their locations. Clarify this and make sure you know where all the locations are.

Malpractice insurance – Malpractice coverage will normally be paid by the practice. It is recommended that associates carry the same policy their employer carries. If you are self-employed or contracting your services to a hospital or clinic, you will need to provide your own coverage. In this case, inquire as to what insurance company insures the majority of the physicians with that group.

Signing bonus – The amount and size of signing bonuses can vary widely, however, it is important to pay attention to when the bonus is paid. If you sign with your practice in the calendar year prior to your starting date, make sure you get your bonus in the year prior to starting practice. By getting the bonus in the prior calendar year, you will owe less in taxes on the bonus, since your income will be lower.

Other benefits – If you are in a group practice with many owners, it is common to have some group life, health, and disability insurance, as well as a 401(k) plan. If you are working at a small private practice, you would most likely cover those expenses on your own. It is also helpful if the private practice has a qualified retirement plan available for you. Clarifying vacation time and continuing medical education are also important to discuss to avoid misunderstanding.

The Pros and Cons of Large Group Practices Versus Private Practice

Working with hundreds of physicians, we receive significant feedback from our clients as to what they like and dislike about their situation. If you have an entrepreneurial spirit and like the challenge of running a business, the private practice route may be the best situation. For those who would rather not have to deal with these things and want a little more security and stability, a group practice will be attractive. Deciding which fits you best and then going that route will make you the most satisfied professionally. Here is a brief summary of the issues based on our experience.

The benefits of a large group practice are as follows:

- Solid group benefits, including life insurance, disability insurance, health insurance, malpractice insurance, as well as a qualified retirement plan.
- Consistent salary – Normally large groups offer a base salary that can be increased with production.
- Your responsibility is to provide medical services. You are not required to handle staffing issues, payroll, hiring and firing, etc. So when your work is done, you can go home.
- Your personal risk is lower, since you are not responsible for paying for the expenses of the practice.
- You share emergency calls with others in your group.

The drawbacks to large group practices include:

- In the long run, your income can be lower than owning a private practice.
- You have less control over your hours.

- You may have less control over patient care, especially if you accept a lot of insurance.
- You have no asset to sell when you want to leave if you do not buy in.

We see the following advantages in private practice:

- You have a higher potential income.
- You have complete control over how you practice. You decide what you want to focus on and what insurance you will accept.
- You have flexibility in what hours and what days you will be open.
- You are building an asset to sell at retirement.

The drawbacks of private practice include:

- You have higher personal risk. You are now responsible for paying for the practice, building, salaries, supplies, etc.
- You are responsible for the hiring, firing, and staffing issues or you can pay someone to do it.
- You will generally not have employer-offered life or disability insurance.
- You need to provide your own retirement plan.
- You must coordinate emergency call coverage when you are out of town.

The military also offers some competitive options. Typically, the government will pay for a large portion of your school costs. In return, you must practice in a branch of the armed services for a specified number of years when you complete school or residency. While the pay is lower than a private or group practice, your student loans are less, your medical care is covered, and you receive a housing allowance. If you have flexibility in where you live for a few years after graduation, this can be a great option.

Moonlighting

In many ways, moonlighting at an offsite facility can be very similar to operating a private practice. If the hospital or clinic you contract your services to gives you a 1099, then you are considered self-employed. If they give you a W2, then you are an employee. Working as an employee requires no additional work on your end. Your taxes will be withheld and your FICA taxes will be paid.

If you get a 1099, this gives you tremendous opportunities to deduct reasonable business expenses and reduce your taxation. Reasonable business expenses can be business travel, CME expenses, dues, publications, professional fees, automobile expenses, cell phone, laptop, medical equipment, food, or entertainment. If you do receive a 1099, it is wise to consult with your accountant or a financial advisor familiar with moonlighting income.

It is very important to understand that if no taxes are being withheld from your checks, you should set aside at least 45 percent of your moonlighting check for taxes. This money should be kept in a separate money market or savings account. As an independent contractor, your income taxes will be higher than as an employee. This is because you must pay both sides of the FICA tax, which equals 15.3 percent, compared to 7.65 percent as an employee. This, added to the 30 percent you could already be paying, can push your effective tax rate on moonlighting income to 45 percent or higher. This is why it is important to keep track of your expenses and be organized.

It is also possible to set up a specific retirement plan for 1099 income. The most common examples would be a SEP IRA or Simple IRA discussed in Chapter Eight. These allow you to put the income aside before federal and state taxes are paid. Most physicians moonlight to make money to spend, but if you are concerned about taxes or retirement, setting up a SEP IRA or Simple IRA could make sense.

Deciding whether to incorporate is also something you may want to consider. If you are concerned about being sued or are in a high risk specialty, setting up a professional association, S corporation, or LLC may make sense. This will limit your liability. However, most independent contractors will be covered by the malpractice insurance of the practice they are moonlighting at. In addition, most young physicians have relatively few assets and are not an attractive target for a lawsuit.

As a physician, you have so many choices as to how you can practice. The key is finding the method that is fulfilling and rewarding to you, both professionally and personally. This gives you the opportunity to serve your community in many ways.

11

Conclusion

The medical profession is a wonderful career choice. It offers flexibility in how, what, when, and where you want to practice. The combination of these factors give you so many financial choices. The decisions you make financially should be based on your own personal and business goals. What makes sense for a friend's career may not make sense for you. The type of college savings plan you set up may be different than your neighbor's. The life insurance you choose may not be the same as your business partner's if you have different life goals or cash flow. The decisions you make need to be based on what *you* value most in life.

A successful financial plan should work under all scenarios, things that occur in real life. In the event that you live a long, healthy life, you want your plan to provide income to you throughout retirement and maintain your lifestyle. If, unfortunately, things do not go as planned, your financial plan should protect you, your family, your employees, and your assets. The plan should work to accomplish your goals as effectively as possible. This means growing your net worth efficiently, enjoying life, minimizing taxes, and managing your risks. A good financial plan will not only address the financial aspects of your life, but will also provide valuable piece of mind.

Having a properly designed financial plan and a relationship with a trusted financial planner will be a source of comfort and strength. The peace of mind in knowing you have planned for all contingencies is not something that can be quantified in dollars. It is something that can only be experienced. We hope this book gives you the information you need to start putting your financial affairs in order or finish what you may have already started.

12

Additional Resources

Glossary of Financial Terms

Annuities, Fixed	An investment marketed by an insurance company that pays a guaranteed rate of return.
Annuity, Variable	An investment marketed by an insurance company with premiums mostly converted into separate accounts invested in stocks, bonds, and money market accounts.
Assets	An investment or property that has value.
Fixed Assets	Those assets that do not have a major loss of principal. These would include the most conservative assets in your portfolio, like checking and savings accounts, money market funds, certificates of deposit, T-bills, EE savings bonds, whole life insurance cash values, etc.
"Bear" Market	A period of time in which securities are declining in price.
"Bull" Market	A period of time in which securities are rising in price.
Capital	Money or other assets.

Certificate of Deposit	An account at a bank, savings and loan, and/or credit union that pays a fixed rate over a certain period of time.
CFP	Certified financial planner – A person who advises others on achieving long-term financial goals, either for a fee or on a commission basis. Ethics and professional standards are monitored by the CFP Board: www.cfp-board.org.
ChFC	Chartered financial consultant – A degree emphasizing investments and tax planning earned through the American College.
CLU	Chartered life underwriter – A degree in insurance and risk management earned though the American College.
Debt	Owing money.
Deferment	A six-month grace period granted to federal student loans at the conclusion of medical school. Economic hardship deferment can be offered after your initial deferment if you qualify financially. If you qualify, your loans can remain in deferment for up to another three years. During any deferment, only your unsubsidized loans accrue interest.
Diversification	Spreading your risk among various accounts to reduce volatility.
Dollar Cost Averaging	The buying of a fixed dollar amount of stock shares at regular intervals so that more shares are bought at low prices, fewer at high, resulting in an average cost that is lower than the average price.

Forbearance	A declaration of non-payment that must be granted to residents and fellows during training. During forbearance, all your loans will accrue interest.
IRA	Individual retirement account.
Liquidity	How easy it is to convert your investment into cash.
Money Market Mutual Fund	A pool of assets invested in bank CDs, T-bills, and commercial paper, and considered the best emergency reserve account due to extreme safety and liquidity.
Portfolio	A listing of securities held by an investor or organization.
Principal	The current balance owed on a debt or the value of an account.
MSFS	Master of financial services – An advanced degree earned by the American College.
Mutual Fund	A general term for an open-end investment company compromised of investments in basically any category.
Subsidized Loan	A federal loan where the interest during school and deferment is not accruing.
Securities	Investments.
Sales Load	An upfront fee or commission on a mutual fund purchase used to compensate the broker or financial planner.
Stock/Share	A certificate representing ownership in a corporation that is usually sold to raise money to begin or expand a business.

| T-Bills | Treasury bill – A short-term federal obligation of the United States Treasury sold at a discount. |
| Unsubsidized Loan | A loan that accrues interest during school and training. |

For Further Information

The following is a very brief list of some of the resources for the individual interested in personal financial planning. To list all the helpful information available today would be a book in itself, so included here are some of the most popular, and our personal favorites. The opinions and strategies expressed in the following sources should not be acted upon without first discussing them with a qualified investment, tax, and/or legal advisor.

Newspapers

The Wall Street Journal is the most widely read business newspaper. It also has daily articles about investing and money matters.

Barron's is a weekly newspaper that reviews the stock markets. The Lipper Analytical Services mutual fund performance ratings are included on a quarterly basis. There are also frequent articles on mutual fund investing.

Investor's Business Daily is an excellent newspaper with a broad range of articles on finance, business, and the economy.

New York Times and *USA Today* both have excellent business sections.

Magazines

Medical Economics frequently publishes articles related to financial issues concerning physicians.
Money magazine's December, January, and February issues usually have articles on tax and investment planning.

Kiplinger's Personal Finance magazine's January issue focuses on financial planning (including tax planning) for the coming year. Mutual funds are reviewed in the September issue.

Smart Money offers articles on investing and financial planning.

Forbes is a biweekly investment magazine that looks at news from an investment point of view and has an annual mutual fund survey, usually published in August.

Business Week focuses on current business news and contains articles on personal business, investing, and financial planning.

Books

The New Retirementality by Mitch Anthony is a great new book that identifies the issues facing everyone as they plan their future. This is especially helpful to those who are worried about what they will do during their retirement years.

The Ultimate Gift by Jim Stovall provides a very interesting story about wealth and the transfer of wealth to the next generation. We would suggest this book for anyone who wants to instill a sense of value and work ethic into their children, employees, and others.

Web Sites

www.ama-assn.org is the official Web site for the American Medical Association.

www.bloomberg.com offers financial market reports.

www.investorama.com lists information on thousands of online financial sites.

www.irs.gov provides information on publications and forms to answer most tax questions.

www.marshallgifford.com is co-author Marshall Gifford's Web site and lists his presentations, background, philosophies, and links to other helpful sites.

www.memag.com is the Web site for *Medical Economics Magazine.*

www.morningstar.com features a comprehensive review of mutual funds and portfolio tracking.

www.quicken.com includes a wealth of personal finance information, as well as calculators and interactive financial formulas.

www.savingsbonds.gov lists everything you need to know about United States savings bonds.

www.savingforcollege.com discusses the multitude of state 529 college plans available, and each of their advantages.

www.sec.gov is the official site of the Securities and Exchange Commission.

www.toddbramson.com is Todd's Web site and lists his presentations, e-newsletter, and many excellent links.

www.wallstreetcity.com has just about everything you need to know about stocks, including free quotes, research, and criteria-based charts matching your specifications.

Variable life insurance, variable annuities, and mutual funds are sold only by prospectus. The prospectus contains important information about the product's charges and expenses, as well as the risks and other information associated with the product. You should carefully consider the risks and investment charges of a specific product before investing. You should always read the prospectus carefully before investing.

This book contains a lot of information and investment/planning strategies. Keeping in mind that everyone's financial situation is different, the strategies and concepts discussed within this book may not be appropriate for everyone. You should meet with your financial, legal, and tax advisor(s) before implementing any financial, legal, or tax strategy.

The tax concepts that are addressed in this book are current as of 2005. Tax laws change frequently, and any tax concept addressed in this book may not be applicable after 2005.

Specific tax consequences addressing 529 college savings plans, dividends, and capital gain are all subject to a sunset provision. Unless these are signed into permanent law, the favorable tax provisions are subject to expire between January of 2008 and December 31, 2010.

Todd D. Bramson and Marshall W. Gifford and are registered representatives with CRI Securities, Inc.

0716-2004-12149

DOFU: 09/05

ABOUT THE AUTHORS

Certified financial planner Todd D. Bramson has been working in the field of financial planning for over twenty years, and has been recognized as one of the 150 best financial advisors for doctors nationwide by *Medical Economics Magazine*. He is one of only a few financial advisors who have been listed each time *Medical Economics* has provided this survey. An exceptional teacher, as well as a motivating author and speaker, he has been quoted in numerous financial publications, and has spent several years as the financial expert on the local NBC live 5:00 p.m. news broadcast. In June of 2004, he spoke at the prestigious Million Dollar Round Table, a worldwide organization of the top one half of one percent of all financial services professionals. He writes an e-newsletter, *The Bramson Report*, and maintains a Web site at www.toddbramson.com.

Mr. Bramson is also a member of the very exclusive Wealth Protection Alliance. This nationwide association of attorneys, accountants, and financial advisors are dedicated to educating and implementing cutting-edge strategies on asset protection and wealth protections.

Mr. Bramson's belief, "If the trust is there, the miles don't matter," has earned him devoted clients not only in his hometown of Madison, Wisconsin, but in almost every state in the country. Along with all the advanced degrees expected of a trusted financial professional, he is committed to keeping abreast of all the developments in his field, and to playing an active role in his community. Mr. Bramson conducts regular public seminars and is active in his church, the Breakfast Optimist Club, Evans Scholars Alumni Foundation, and Blackhawk Country Club.

Mr. Bramson is also the founder and president of Bramson and Associates LLC. Information on his company, philosophy, and services can be found at www.toddbramson.com. You will quickly see that Mr. Bramson is dedicated to providing valuable wisdom through his books, Web site, presentations, and newsletters.

Chartered financial consultant Marshall Gifford has been working as a financial advisor in Minneapolis, Minnesota, since 1993 and consults with clients who reside across the country. He has specialized in working with physicians since 1993. Since 1993, Mr. Gifford has worked extensively with graduates of the University of Minnesota Medical School and residency programs, as well as the residency and fellowship programs at the Mayo Clinic. He also works with physicians at hundreds of private practices across the United States. He prides himself on keeping current on trends in medicine.

Mr. Gifford's financial advice has been quoted in numerous financial publications, and he has appeared on Twin Cities news stations numerous times as a financial expert. He is a member of the Court of the Table, reserved for the top one half of one percent of financial advisors worldwide.

Mr. Gifford is also President and founder of M.W. Gifford Consulting LLC, that offers timely information and financial presentations to physician groups and residency programs. His Web site can be accessed at www.marshallgifford.com.

Mr. Gifford is an avid athlete. He enjoys cycling, running, cross-country skiing, and wakeboarding. He played basketball for Minnesota State University, Mankato, and was also ninth in the country in the decathlon in 1993. He has ridden RAGBRAI, the *Des Moines Register*'s annual bike ride across Iowa, every year since 1990, and he ran the Boston Marathon in 2003.

Mr. Gifford lives in St. Paul, Minnesota, with his wife and two sons.

 North Star Resource Group

Marathon Advisors, Inc. – *Investment Advisor Representative*
Registered Investment Advisor

Todd D. Bramson, CFP, CLU, ChFC
North Star Resource Group
2945 Triverton Pike Drive #200
Madison, WI 53711
1-608-271-9100 ext. 218
todd.bramson@northstarfinancial.com

Marshall W. Gifford, CLU, ChFC
North Star Resource Group
2701 University Avenue SE
Minneapolis, MN 55414
1-612-617-6119 or 1-888-257-9839
marshall.gifford@northstarfinancial.com

Management
Best Sellers

Visit Your Local Bookseller Today or Go to
www.Aspatore.com for More Information

- <u>Corporate Ethics</u> - Making Sure You are in Compliance with Ethics Policies; How to Update/Develop an Ethics Plan for Your Team - $17.95

- <u>10 Technologies Every Executive Should Know</u> - Executive Summaries of the Ten Most Important Technologies Shaping the Economy - $17.95

- <u>The Board of the 21st Century</u> - Board Members from Wal-Mart, Philip Morris, and More on Avoiding Liabilities and Achieving Success in the Boardroom - $27.95

- <u>Inside the Minds: Leading CEOs</u> - CEOs from Office Max, Duke Energy, and More on Management, Leadership, and Profiting in Any Economy - $27.95

- <u>Deal Teams</u> - Roles and Motivations of Management Team Members, Investment Bankers, Professional Services Firms, Lawyers, and More in Doing Deals (Partnerships, M&A, Equity Investments) - $27.95

- <u>The Governance Game</u> - What Every Board Member and Corporate Director Should Know About What Went Wrong in Corporate America and What New Responsibilities They are Faced With - $24.95

- <u>Smart Business Growth</u> - Leading CEOs on Twelve Ways to Increase Revenues and Profits for Your Team/Company - $27.95

- CEO Profit Centers – Top CEOs on Key Strategies for Increasing Profits Exponentially in any Economy - $27.95

**Buy All 8 Titles Above and
Save 40% - Only $131.75**

Call 1-866-Aspatore (277-2867) to Order

Other Best Sellers

Visit Your Local Bookseller Today or Go to
www.Aspatore.com for More Information

- The Golf Course Locator for Business Professionals – Golf Courses Closest to Largest Companies, Law Firms, Cities, and Airports, 180 Pages, $12.95

- Deal Teams - Roles and Motivations of Management Team Members, Venture Capitalists, Investment Bankers, Lawyers, and More in Mergers, Acquisitions, and Equity Investments - $27.95

- 10 Technologies Every Executive Should Know - Executive Summaries of the Ten Most Important Technologies Shaping the Economy - $17.95

- Software Agreements Line by Line - How to Understand and Change Software Licenses and Contracts to Fit Your Needs - $49.95

- Business Travel Bible – Must-Have Phone Numbers, Business Resources, and Maps, 240 Pages, $14.95

- Living Longer, Working Stronger – Simple Steps for Business Professionals to Capitalize on Better Health, 160 Pages, $14.95

- Business Grammar, Style, and Usage – Rules for Articulate and Polished Business Writing and Speaking, 100 Pages, $14.95

- ExecRecs – Executive Recommendations for the Best Business Products and Services, 140 Pages, $14.95

- Executive Adventures – More than Fifty Exhilarating Out-of-the-Office Escape Vacations, 100 Pages, $14.95

- The C-Level Test – Business IQ and Personality Test for Professionals of All Levels, 60 Pages, $17.95

- The Business Translator – Business Words, Phrases, and Customs in Over Sixty-Five Languages, 540 Pages, $29.95

- Term Sheets & Valuations (CD-ROM - Customizable) - Includes an NDA, Due Diligence Checklist, and Term Sheet (from Above Book) in a Word Doc that Can be Customized - $49.95